The Liturgy of Pastoral Care:

A worship shaped ministry of care

The Liturgy of Pastoral Care:

A worship shaped ministry of care

John David Connolly

A Self-Published Work

Unless otherwise stated, all biblical references are quoted from the New Revised Standard Version (NRSV) (Division of Christian Education of the National Council of the Churches of Christ in the United States of America, 1989)

The views and opinions expressed in this book belong solely to the author and in no way represent the views of the US Navy, the US Navy Chaplain Corps, or the Evangelical Lutheran Church in America.

First Printing: 2020

Paperback ISBN 978-1-7348393-3-3

eBook ISBN 978-1-7348393-2-6

Published by John David Connolly

Interior and cover graphics design by Maggie Connolly

Contents

Dedication

To Peter,

who challenged me to realize my call from God,

and refused to take "No" for an answer.

To Tony,

who first gave me the vocabulary of WIGIAT,

and awareness of God with us in our pastoral care.

To Kim, Michael, Jeffrey, Jon, and David

who pushed me to take on the mantle of chaplain,

and would not accept mediocrity.

To Emma,

who is my beloved,

and continuously encourages me in all my endeavors.

To Maggie,

who is absolutely my pride and joy,

and who inspires me to always enjoy my inner child.

I love and thank you all!

Introduction

Pastoral care is at the heart of the compassion of the pastor, priest, rabbi, imam, or whatever title clergy may go by. To extend care in connection with our faith and the faith of those for whom we care while they are in some moment of crisis or need is what sets clergy apart from other helping professionals. We are not trying to heal their bodies as much as we are extending care that brings peace to their souls, often allowing the healing to flow to their bodies as well. It is in this moment of extending care where our faith as clergy and their faith of those in need intersect in a moment of intimate healing for both. The key to this care is love; love for our neighbors by extending ourselves into their moments of pain or struggle and intentionally exposing ourselves to their pain so we can bring them healing in a spiritual way.

Venturing through the educational and academic process of Clinical Pastoral Education (CPE) I found it to be a very contemplative and reflective time for me personally that broadened my understanding and application of pastoral care immensely. This process pushed and challenged me to think in ways I never have regarding how effective pastoral care can be provided, not to mention how ineffective we can also be if care is not taken in our interactions with those seeking care from us. A revelation for me from my CPE experience is how I now see the application of pastoral care, or how we as pastors tend to people in need emotionally and spiritually, from a different perspective.

One of the significant epiphanies I experienced is my awareness of myself so I could be the most for the other while endeavoring to prevent myself from polluting the encounter needed by the one for whom I am caring.

Through this season of my life, I contemplated my own theological underpinning as well as my application of pastoral care and how best to provide it. What I mean by this is I looked more deeply into my own understanding of God, and who I am in relationship with God. I looked deeply into my call and my ordination which continually provide guidance in my current ministry setting. I had to reflect deeply on the genuineness of my sense of call to this particular ministry, which is not just for anyone.

As a Lutheran pastor I have a certain understanding of who God is and who I am in relationship to God that informs every aspect of my being; not the least of which is my role as clergy. I have found this understanding comforting and reassuring in this journey. In the midst of a very pluralistic and diverse religious (and even non-religious) environment of working as a military and a hospital chaplain, it often feels like you need to forgo strict adherence to your own theological DNA to adopt a least common denominator approach to ministry, but nothing could be further from the truth. What I have discovered is I can be me and be consistent with the sense of call with which I believe and feel God has called me without the need to water down my ministry or my theology to the least common denominator. I do not have to compromise who I am nor how I best relate to God in order to care for someone who may have a different understanding or relationship with God; neither do they need to compromise their relationship with God on my behalf. We have the opportunity to be genuine with each other in our own unique relationships with God, and grow and heal from that encounter – both of us.

As a Lutheran pastor and chaplain, I identify with and am very comfortable with worship that is liturgical in nature. What this means is there is a traditional flow to worship which provides a structure that is more or less consistent from congregation to congregation and week to week. Although there will certainly be some variation, there are certain elements and patterns that can reasonably be expected from one service to the next. This sense of pattern and consistency that we refer to as liturgical worship is not unique to Lutherans. Episcopalians, Catholics, Methodists, Anglicans, and many other Christian traditions would also be considered liturgical in their worship style, which is unique to that particular faith group. Even for faith traditions that refer to themselves as non-liturgical they too have a certain flow to their worship which is consistent and comfortable for them. This liturgy, or order of worship, provides the framework for a dialogue of worship, praise, and prayer between the pastor, the congregation, and God. The liturgy or structure to the worship service would also extend to faith traditions like Jewish or Muslim or other non-Christian traditions as they gather for worship or prayers with their consistent patterns of worship. Yet, even traditions more individualistic and solitary in their practice like some Buddhist or Native American traditions would also have a certain pattern to private or individual devotional and worship practices; or a liturgy of their own.

An epiphany to me was the fact that there is also a pattern in the provision of pastoral care; a liturgy, if you will. There is a dialogue formed around a chaplain and a patient, or family, or friends, or staff, and God that also has a form and structure to it comparable to the structure which exists in the typical worship environment. This structure has a certain consistency to it from person to person. This structure or liturgy can be a source of comfort to the chaplain and the patient (or others involved) where they find it familiar and peaceful as a place to explore those spiritual wounds and begin to find healing for them.

This book or project is an exploration of the liturgy that develops around pastoral care; what shape it takes, and what is typically present. As with liturgy in worship, it has a defined beginning, middle, and end which equips the faithful to go out in service in God's name or even just continue on the path we are on in the presence of God with God's peace. I contend that realizing and appreciating this liturgy will remind us of the importance of each component of a pastoral care encounter. No single component of this liturgy is more or less important than any other component of our encounter with a patient, family member, staff member, or any other person to whom we extend our care. It is also helpful to remember that, as with worship in a typical congregational setting, the presiding clergy is also part of the worship; he or she is not detached from it. Therefore, as the pastoral care provider, we are also part of this worship as we walk

6

through the liturgy of pastoral care with those whom we encounter; we simply have a unique role that we are set apart for and called into. Finally, and probably most importantly, with the understanding of our pastoral encounters as a worshipping encounter, we are reminded of the fact that God is not absent from the encounter. In fact, our encounter occurs looking to God as our source of comfort and healing as well as the rightful recipient of our praise and adoration. It is in God we find all healing, and it is in God's name we gather, even in a hospital room.

Although the term "patient" and other medically related terms are used, I encourage us all to consider every encounter in this light. We may be encountering a prisoner, an assault victim, a community leader seeking guidance, or a spouse struggling with their marriage. Yet, every encounter is an opportunity to experience and represent the holy. Every encounter is to encounter God in our midst. Every encounter is an opportunity, together with the people we are called to serve, to praise and worship God. And, there is a pattern each clergy adopts in providing that care, that worship. This is the liturgy of our pastoral care.

What is Pastoral Care?

Each day, I spend time with the people of God in a variety of ways. I enter the places they are and I spend time with them in their setting in life. It may be in their workplace, their home, their hospital room, their prison cell, or any of a dozen or more other places. The physical location or setting doesn't matter, but it does at the same time. It matters because it matters to these wonderful people of God, but it doesn't make any difference in my desire to be with them on life's journey.

The part of this that truly matters is the time; my time is given to them as a gift. In pastoral care, the greatest gift we have to give is ourselves and our time for the people who are the recipients of our care. Medical professionals, financial advisors, funeral home directors, etc. all have to conduct their dealings with an individual based on an agenda centered in a cost versus profit analysis; pastors do not. The pastor's agenda is attending to the person as a child of God and nothing else. The pastor, intentionally, sets aside all other concerns to dedicate that moment in time to the person and the person's spiritual well-being. In short, we are their servants, and we are honored and humbled to have that calling in our lives.

In other helping professions, such as medical, the doctor would use a wide array of diagnostic techniques to determine the ailment of a patient and prescribe a treatment to affect healing. In pastoral care, we approach it much more broadly. We do not use diagnostic tools to ascertain an affliction or ailment of some form; the person simply tells us their concerns. Our main discernment on their behalf is to determine and reflect the presence of God already present and real in their lives in such a way that they can witness it themselves; to reflect the fact that God is with them. By and large, we do not prescribe any treatment regimen to affect change; we are simply with the person. From a theological perspective, any diagnosis or prescribed treatment regimen would be a gift from the Holy Spirit to their spirit; the pastor is simply there to shepherd and witness that process.

In fairness, there is something akin to a diagnosis we provide, but we approach it differently from other helping professionals. The occasion for which we are visiting with the person may be one of grief, shame, guilt, joy, or any number of other concerns; but the person self-diagnoses that reality. The occasion may be one of joy, elation, or celebration; on those occasions, we are invited to join the celebration. The occasion may be one of searching, confusion, or discernment; and again, the person for whom we are caring is the one that defines their own "diagnosis".

We simply affirm it with them and help them to process their own diagnosis. The other side of this, however, is one where the person is truly at a crossroads or conundrum and seeking guidance. On these occasions, the pastor will often provide the diagnosis of truth, which may be painful but necessary for spiritual healing. Usually, on these occasions, the person for whom we care is already aware of the circumstance but relies on the pastor to help them to say it out loud.

To provide this level of honesty, pastoral care necessarily begins with a relationship. The relationship stems from one of trust that allows the pastor, the priest, the rabbi, the imam, or the chaplain to enter into the lives of the people they care for in a most intimate, emotional, and spiritual way. Because of the trust, the individual is free to share their joys, their sorrows, their griefs, their successes, and their shames without judgment or recrimination. The pastoral caregiver is there representing the holy, although all are fully aware the pastoral caregiver is no more or less holy than the person they care for. The pastoral caregiver may be in a worse position personally than the person for whom they care. Yet, in their role as a pastoral caregiver, they stand in a position called to care for others despite any blemishes they may have themselves.

The pastoral caregiver's greatest responsibilities begin with making a safe place for individuals to share what weighs on them, and to receive what is shared with them in a way that brings healing. Through this, the recipient of the care and the care provider experience healing they both need as this burden is offloaded through the exchange between individual and pastoral caregiver.

To make a safe place for sharing involves the physical space, but it also the emotional and spiritual space. The physical space, in an ideal world, should be closed off from hearing, but not from view. What is meant by this is those outside the space, created by the pastor, others would not be able to hear what is said or shared between the pastor and the person to whom he or she is extending care, but with a casual and non-intrusive glance it can be discerned physical safety is maintained. This could take the form of an office or conference room, it could be a prison cell or chapel, it could even be in the middle of a field with sufficient distance so others may not hear.

I have had conversations that began in the middle of a passageway or a sidewalk, offices or grassy fields where rifle qualification shooting was taking place. Many conversations are casual and simply passing the time of day, but others go much deeper. On the occasions where the conversation tended to move toward more intimate content and potentially emotional subjects, I found ways to help the person move to a more private location, out of respect for them and the sanctity of the conversation that was beginning to take shape. Yet, rarely did I know which direction the conversation would go before it began; my assumptions and preconceived notions of which path a conversation will take rarely prove to be accurate or very helpful. I've simply found it helpful to remain flexible and open no matter how innocuous a conversation may begin. I have to be a vessel that is open to whatever may be poured into me and cherish what is offered as sacred and holy.

The other aspect of protecting the sanctity of the conversation physically is transparency. Although it is desired to have the conversation audibly completely unheard, it is equally desired to have the visual components completely transparent. On too many occasions, in too many places and situations, accusations and/or realities of inappropriate clergy contact with those whom he or she is charged has taken place. Speaking in the open, or in a room with a window, or other venues where others can easily see the actions of the pastor severely curtails the likelihood of any misconduct in the actions of either the pastor or the person they are caring for; it brings what is dark into the light. Not taking care to ensure the visual transparency will continue to erode the sacred trust given to clergy of all faith backgrounds, and, as a result, will completely compromise the care that could have been provided because it will not be trusted, sought, or received.

Emotionally safe spaces are probably even more important than physically safe ones. An emotionally safe space implies an intense level of trust between the person and the pastor. The person simply knows their pastoral care provider will not harm them, violate their trust, and is emotionally present with them. The person knows the pastoral care provider will not ridicule them, but also trusts the pastoral care provider will be completely honest with them even if it may be painful. They come to the pastor because they believe it is a safe place to fully process their deepest emotions and feelings, even if others may think those emotions or feelings are wrong. In other words, the emotionally safe place is a place where the individual can be genuinely themselves and not hide who they are. Theologically speaking, the pastor provides a place of light that is healing and restorative to the individual's place of darkness that they bring into the space, exposing it to the light and finding healing.

To create an emotionally safe place requires the pastoral care provider to be self-aware, non-judgmental, and emotionally present. Depending on what is shared with a pastoral care provider fulfilling these may be the most challenging part of that sacred calling. Our natural tendencies are to be narcissistic, judgmental, and emotionally absent. To not fall prey to these tendencies requires intentionality and discipline.

Self-awareness should recognize our tendencies toward narcissism, our own emotional/spiritual baggage, our biases and prejudices, our own theology, or anything else that could compromise our pastoral care encounter. This self-awareness is not easy. It requires us to know and acknowledge the less attractive parts of ourselves; and even if we don't want to admit it, we all have them. This awareness does not definitively prevent the influence of things we would rather not acknowledge, but it certainly helps us to control them so they do not become a hindrance to those for whom we are caring.

An oversimplification of narcissism is the tendency to say, "It is all about me," or turn everything around to be about one's self. We love to toot our own horn and tell our own story, and at the right time that is perfectly appropriate. But, never is it appropriate when we are caring for another person. The pastor must repress this tendency, even to the level of allowing the person we are caring for to be as narcissistic as they may desire. Their story, not ours, must take center stage. To chime in with our story of woe, grief, pain, shame, or others is by and large not very helpful at all; it tends to shut down the conversation. It doesn't create an emotionally safe space because we convey through our narcissism we do not care about the needs of the person we are supposedly caring for, and instead, try to turn them into our pastor; it turns the relationship upside down and no one experiences the healing they need or desire. If the pastoral care provider needs a chaplain or counselor then he or she should seek out one of their own.

In the healthy pastoral care relationship, the pastor should reach a point he or she can share "of themselves, but not about themselves."[1] This is the healthy balance where we rein in our narcissistic tendencies but can share an appropriate amount "of ourselves" so we can encourage, motivate, or console a person for whom we provide care. Perhaps even the awareness of our narcissistic tendencies can help us internally to better connect and identify with others, but only when we do not impose it on others. Instead, it becomes a lens that helps us to focus and see the challenges others may face. The unhealthy balance is when sharing becomes more "about ourselves" than it is the person we are caring for; that is when we harm instead of help. Mastering this balance will take the pastoral care provider the balance of their lives, and they rarely will get it perfect. But, self-discipline and self-awareness will help us, even with too much sharing, to also provide self-correction to again turn the conversation back to the person who needs our care and away from ourselves. An example would be when a person we are caring for expresses anger or fear, and we experience the same from their situation it would not be inappropriate to share the fact that we have a common emotion, and would be an example of sharing "of ourselves". However, if we were to delve deeply into our past and share the fact that our anger comes from the abusive relationship we had with a parent or a spouse and share the details then we have certainly crossed the line into sharing "about ourselves".

Each of us has unique backgrounds, experiences, hurts, shames, griefs, etc. Connected with each of these are emotions, which are neither good nor bad, but simply are. Our self-awareness would guide us to not allow our own emotions to cloud or color the pastoral care encounter, but preferably to bring even greater healing. Our awareness of what is happening inside us, our emotions and feelings, can help us to understand and better appreciate what the person receiving our care is feeling. It can also help us to be more empathetic and sympathetic to their experiences. When we carry our care to its best and fullest intent we can help guide those for whom we care to healing, not by hiding our hurts but by acknowledging them.

Henri Nouwen described the role of the pastoral caregiver using the metaphor of hospitality and loneliness as a source for healing. He said, "The minister who has come to terms with his own loneliness and is at home in his own house is a host who offers hospitality to his guests. He gives them a friendly space, where they may feel free to come and go, to be close and distant, to rest and to play, to talk and to be silent, to eat and to fast...It is healing because it does not take away the loneliness and the pain of another, but invites him to recognize his loneliness on a level where it can be shared."[2] The wound is therefore not shared in some salacious way bringing attention to the care provider alone, but in a way that allows for healing for all.

Looking at our own biases and prejudices can often feel like looking at our own excrement. To deny we have any biases or prejudices is also much akin to denying any of us have bowel movements, or to deny the results of the bowl movement smells awful; we all have them and they always stink, period. However, just as we have a proper place for our excrement there is also a proper place for our biases and prejudices. They are not there to be center stage in the conversation with those for whom we care, but we need to be aware of them so they do not take center stage and impede our provision of care. Imposing them on those we care for would be on par with having our excrement in the middle of our dining room table; completely inappropriate and unpleasant.

One of the problems, however, with biases and prejudices is the fact we often don't realize how biased or prejudiced we are. Most of us only come to that realization when we are confronted with it by someone we trust or even in a more compromising situation. We may be sexist, racist, ageist, or any of several other biases or prejudices. Imagine, in a pastoral care role you are responsible for providing care for someone from an ethnic background you have significant biases towards. First, your bias would most likely be very evident to the person for whom you are caring and trust would not be possible. Second, your bias would tend to cause you to make assumptions about the individual based on your feelings for their ethnicity without seeing and treating them as an individual in their own right. Third, any reflections or recommendations you have would most likely not be centered in love and for what is best for the person, but instead closer to what is best for you or even a detriment to them is. A relationship that begins with a lack of trust and broad assumptions not based on fact will prove to not only be not helpful but quite possibly hurtful and cause further harm to the person.

Biases do tend to go the other way as well. On one particular visit while serving in a hospital setting I had a patient immediately excuse me, in no uncertain terms, from his room as soon as he saw my clerical collar and I introduced myself as his chaplain. I did pause momentarily to ask him why he was summarily dismissing me without knowing anything about me. His response, "People like you don't care about people like me and all you do is judge me." "Like me?" I replied. "Yes, pastors and priests don't accept me for who I am," he rebutted. The conversation still haunts me to this day. I honored his demand to leave his room, but I still grieve the loss. Because of the biases of some clergy he had encountered before I met him, he developed a strong, protective bias of his own, including those who would not judge him. With perhaps more experience I could have still created a safe spiritual space for him, but on that day I was not able to. The loss of that opportunity was his, mine, and ours.

As an emotional aside from the previous example, I am reminded of the damage that has been done by some clergy members who place one perceived sin as greater than another. As a result, they refuse to provide care to one such "sinner" until they change their ways and become "righteous". The effect of this approach has driven many from faith altogether, rather than draw them toward the God who loves them. This excommunicates the individual from a faith connection from which they could experience healing, love, forgiveness, and growth. I encourage clergy, of all traditions, if you encounter an individual that you cannot, in good conscience, counsel or provide care to then please connect them with another who will.

Our ability to be emotionally present will, in many encounters, push us to our limits. Our emotional presence begins with genuinely loving and caring for the person for whom we are providing care, no matter what. It is easy to love a tender, newborn baby and its mother still in the glow of new life. To love a sociopathic, non-repentant, murderer is another thing altogether; it requires all the emotional and spiritual fortitude we have.

To love a sinner, in the broadest sense of the word, in no way condones their sins. Paul proclaimed to the Corinthian church, "Love is patient; love is kind; love is not envious or boastful or arrogant or rude. It does not insist on its own way; it is not irritable or resentful; it does not rejoice in wrongdoing, but rejoices in the truth. It bears all things, believes all things, hopes all things, endures all things."[3] Our emotional presence will not deny the anger, grief, guilt, or shame we may feel based on their

18

actions and attitude. Instead, we embrace those feelings in such a way we are informed by them but not controlled by them. We choose to be patient and kind, even in the face of evil. We choose to endure all things so that, in the end, we provide a safe pastoral care space, where, in time, the person may come to a place where spiritual healing can take place. In our patience, kindness, and endurance we provide a safe venue where the individual could come to a place of trust of not only us but also the God we serve. Through our actions, we have the opportunity to be the catalyst toward reconciliation with the community, with God and with themselves. But, we must first love them, no matter what.

Our emotional presence also encourages us to not be controlled by, but be aware of our own feelings and emotions. When we can tap into those emotions during an encounter with a person we have the opportunity to become aware of what they may be feeling or experiencing. We then have the chance to speak with the individual about their feelings, hurts, longings, pains, etc., and to be an agent of healing and hope through our sensitivities and awareness. This can become too much, however, if we experience sadness and the person we are supposed to be caring for is consoling us rather than the other way around. It certainly takes time and discipline to not allow your neuroses to complicate the pastoral care encounter, while still allowing your own emotions to be present as a guide to you.

Pastoral care is thus encountering one of God's children to care for them based on faith. This is based on your faith background and journey as you encounter another who

19

experiences their faith background and journey. It is not an effort to change or convert them, but to allow the God in whom we all trust to bring healing in body, mind, and soul by allowing an open space in our hearts and minds for God to act. Pastoral care is not so much a proclamational ministry as it is an incarnational ministry; one where the pastor helps the one being cared for realize the abiding presence of God already in that space and available for them by standing in that space with them. The chaplain could be Christian, Jewish, Muslim, Buddhist, or some other faith tradition and the reality of this helping ministry remains the same. It eventually becomes an opportunity where together, the chaplain and the person, encounter the presence of God. The chaplain, through word and action, introduces the presence of the Holy and Sacred to the person by primarily allowing the person to continue on their faith journey with the chaplain as a companion and perhaps an interpreter or guide. Worship permeates the place and it becomes a holy place and time as this encounter takes place

Although the individual and the chaplain may not think of it in these terms, they have begun to tread upon holy ground and worship takes place. It is not the typical large church, steeple, and four-part-harmony choir, but it is worship nonetheless. It is sacred and should be treated as such.

Pastoral care is thus leaning on the chaplain's faith first. The chaplain's faith is of paramount importance. He or she must believe that God's care and concern are real. They are not to provide false hope or unrealistic expectations, but be able to represent a hope, based on their faith, that transcends the earthly realities to intersect with the divine realities of the chaplain's faith. This is the place of the holy in which the chaplain stands on behalf of those for whom they care.

The chaplain is also secure in their own faith so that they are not threatened by the incongruence of the person's faith they care for with comparison to their own. The chaplain creates a space where both can exist and both can be uplifted and validated by their respective faiths, even if they differ. In short, it is imperative the chaplain fully respects the faith, or even lack of faith, for any who is a recipient of their care.

With this in mind, the chaplain is free to be themselves and not adopt a false persona. In being themselves they represent the place of the holy, even in their brokenness, for any they extend their care to. And, care in this fashion is from the heart and will accomplish much.

This care may take place in a clinical, industrial, religious, or wide variety of other settings. But, this care is unique since it depends on what is sacred to both chaplain and the care recipient to bring healing; not what the chaplain brings or any other human. Healing takes place, shepherded by the chaplain but orchestrated by God through the faith of all present. This is a time of God's presence, with God's people. This is pastoral care, and this is worship.

When Moses encountered the Lord in the burning bush he also encountered holy ground.[4] When he first turned aside to see the burning bush, he did not intentionally embark upon a holy mission but was surprised to find was on holy ground. It was in the Lord's revelation to him that he was indeed standing on holy ground. The holy ground is the incarnational ministry where we encounter the presence of God with us, Emmanuel. When we step into that space where we visit the people we care for we open ourselves to the possibility that we too may be stepping onto holy ground and encountering Emmanuel ourselves. This is where pastoral care becomes the most meaningful to both the patient and the chaplain, and where both are fed and nourished in the sacredness of pastoral care. And, when we realize that we too are standing on holy ground, what better time is there to worship the God who brought us to that place?

Why We Have Pastoral Care?

This is a fair question that is frequently asked. Why do we need pastoral care? Why do we need chaplains and clergy providing pastoral care to people? Shouldn't we spend more money on doctors and nurses instead of chaplains?

From a strictly economic and scientific perspective, pastoral care and clergy will often end up on the chopping block because what we offer is so intangible. We cannot diagnose somatic diseases or psychological disorders. We cannot prescribe treatment regimens or administer them. We cannot do, nor should we do, the vast majority of things that traditional medical professionals do. So, again, why are we there?

Pastoral care and chaplains are there because there are certain things that medicine cannot address, which our spirits can and our spirits need. Through pastoral care and the ministry of chaplains, we address those things, head-on.

Although it is far from a medical or clinical psychological definition, most would agree that depression is, in many ways, the absence of hope. Depression is a mental health disease or disorder that inhibits a person from seeing positive outcomes personally, socially, or on a grander scale.

Depression can result from a clinical diagnosed mental health illness that is unrelated to other life events, or it can occur based on economic, interpersonal relationships, physical health, legal issues, socio-political issues, or many other sources. In essence, any of these or other things becomes a barrier to being able to see or realize hope or even the possibility of hope.

Dr. Don Colbert wrote an incredible book from his perspective, not as a chaplain but a doctor that explored the connection between spiritual health and somatic health. His primary take away, that I agree with wholeheartedly, is the fact that our spiritual/emotional health is very much tied to our physical health; they both affect each other. He mentions, for instance, that, "[in] one thirteen year study, those with major depression had a four-and-a-half times greater risk of heart attack compared to those with no history of depression."[1] This depression is a hopeless situation for the individual that they feel powerless to do anything about, or believe nothing can change their current circumstances.

From a pastoral care perspective, we cannot change the fact that bad things will happen to us. In fact, if you hang around long enough, you will eventually die; that goes for all of us. Despite even that eventuality, however, pastoral care is often about reframing what hope looks like. That reframing is precisely what the pastoral care provider is helping the individual to do so that hope becomes an attainable reality for them.

When reviewing what various practitioners believe are the core tenets of pastoral care I came up with a wide variety of what various experts in pastoral care define as the goals of pastoral care. Many view pastoral care from a more evangelical perspective as a tool or method for conversion or proselytizing. In those cases, pastoral care has a very narrow spectrum that it considers and is seen as a tool, usually, for Christians to make more Christians. I disagree with this as one of the primary goals of pastoral care, although I do agree that with well-intended pastoral care focused on the individual it can occur. With conversion as a primary goal, it puts us in a modality that fails to be concerned with what the individual wants or needs, and, instead, allows the pastoral care provider to determine what is best for the individual.

When you consider the etymology of the word "pastor" you realize its roots stem from shepherding; a pastor is a shepherd. This is why you often hear about a pastor shepherding his or her flock. However, shepherds were never considered to be heartless or single-minded; they care for the sheep according to the sheep's needs. In biblical times, meadows for grazing sheep were often shared or adjoining and not necessarily divided off from one another. If one shepherd came across a sheep in distress he would always care for that sheep, even if it were not from his fold, out of mutual respect for the sheep and the shepherd the sheep actually belonged to. And, the shepherd is not going to try to bring that sheep he helped into his fold; it belongs to another shepherd. This is in the same way that we witness mothers caring for children. No mother would ever ignore a child in need or distress, no matter whose child it is; it is just contrary to a mother's DNA. The mother, will not try to take the child they helped away from its mother; it already has a mother. Pastoral care, in the broadest sense, is very much the same way. When we see a person in need we want to help them through that moment of distress; we are not trying to bring them into our fold. This does not prevent us from sharing the tenets of our faith and what it means to us, but the focus is and should remain on the person and caring for their needs as they express them. In other words, we do not get to define what someone else's needs are, they do. Our calling is to attend to those needs in love without the expectation of anything in return. Anything else is selfishness and is in no way loving or caring.

Henri Nouwen, who died way too early, captured this well in his discussion on hospitality. Our role in pastoral care is really a role of hospitality, even if we are the visitor to their space. He said:

> *Hospitality is not to change people, but to offer them space where change can take place. It is not to bring men and women over to our side, but to to offer freedom not disturbed by dividing lines. It is not to lead our neighbor into a corner where there are*

no alternatives left, but to open a wide spectrum of options for choice and commitment...It is not a method of making our God and our way into the criteria of happiness, but the opening of an opportunity to others to find their God and their way.2

Our care becomes helping the individual connect with their source of hope, but to do that we need to connect with them no matter what "flock" they belong to. We need to get to know them and understand them as a person without trying to make them like us. To try to convince them to leave their own "flock" and join our "flock" without knowing anything about them does not respect them and will make their hope even more distant. When their hope is more distant, so is their health and well-being.

Ultimately, our well-being is connected firmly with our realization of hope, which is often also connected with our faith. Frustratingly, for many chaplains, the faith of the individual they are caring for may or may not match their own, but each person's faith is their own. And, no matter what that faith is, it can and does provide us with hope.

Effectively, every faith tradition that exists has a concept of hope. They are not all alike, but they all help us to connect with something beyond our current situation or reality. I cannot think of any faith tradition that does not have some concept of hope, but they are all unique in what hope may look like.

27

Even within a given faith tradition, hope may be a hard concept to grasp or believe. Although the person may be a strong adherent to that faith tradition, hope may still be allusive. The hope may be allusive because of a chronic or terminal illness. The hope may be allusive because of legal or financial problems that seem insurmountable. Hope may be allusive because the most meaningful relationships have landed on hard times. These are the times that pastoral care becomes the most important because through pastoral care we hear the story, we understand the history, and we shepherd toward their source of hope connected with their faith, and we do this based on our own faith.

Hope is the real currency of pastoral care, and it is purchased through our faith. What we believe and who we believe in is what connects us with our future. The art of pastoral care is to determine what a person believes and who they believe in to provide the currency, and then connect it through their faith to purchase the hope that will preserve them through tough times. When we can do this, we lessen significantly the prevalence of depression in individuals and thus help them enjoy an overall healthier and more satisfying life.

I had an occasion where a patient whom I was caring for was nearing death, and completely nonresponsive. Although his family's faith tradition was very similar to my own and connected with them in a significant way, they all found hope very allusive to grasp onto in any form. It became evident that the patient was not going to recover, which had been their hope. As their chaplain, however, I was able to have a very frank discussion of

28

what hope may look like with his death imminent. It was a painful discussion as I gathered with parents, and siblings, and friends, and others to discuss this new concept of hope. I sat in a room with them as a group and asked them very frankly what hope looked like for them now. For them, even though the life for which they had hoped was no longer realistic, they were able to realize hope as life in others through organ donation. This also connected with their faith as life eternal took on a new meaning for them in those painful hours. Through that connection, pastoral care was able to turn hopeless into hopeful, connected with my faith and the faith of the family.

The reason we provide pastoral care is hope. No procedure that a doctor can provide will provide hope in itself. No medical intervention, or treatment, or anything else from a clinical perspective can provide hope on its own. However, our faith, our own faith, can help us connect with faith that brings hope to bear on hopeless situations. That is exactly the goal of pastoral care, and why ensuring that pastoral care is provided. It is never wasted funds or hours; it helps us find hope where hope did not seem possible. And, with that hope, we find healing in every way imaginable, but without hope life itself can easily lose its meaning.

Dr. Don Colbert discussed very frankly the effect of depression on our physical well-being. My take is eliminating the specter of depression through hope and faith moves us in a direction of health on a more holistic plane. We will never eliminate all of our various woes and troubles, but connected through our faith even those are of no great concern because faith helps us to find hope even beyond the grave.

What is Worship?

Worship is, "reverence and homage, [especially] to God," and in its verbal form, "[to] pay divine honors to; adore (God)."[1] From a dictionary perspective, this may be the accurate definition of worship, but it falls so terribly short to exactly what worship is. This feels like defining diamonds as some shiny rock, or Bach as someone who just happened to play musical instruments. Bach was certainly a musician, and worship is reverence and homage to God. Yet, even the most naïve among us would admit these definitions are simply scratching the surface. There is so much more to Bach, and there is way more to worship.

In Matthew 16 there is a famous conversation between Jesus and his disciples. "[Jesus] asked his disciples, 'Who do people say that the Son of Man is?' And they said, 'Some say John the Baptist, but others Elijah, and still others Jeremiah or one of the prophets.'"[2] I can imagine turning that question around and asking a faithful group of regular worship attendees at nearly any church today, "What do the people say worship is?" My imagined responses would be along the lines of, "Something we have to do, where we meet God, what we do for God, etc." Going further into this story Jesus then turned and asked his disciples, "'[but] who do you say that I am?' Simon Peter answered, 'You are the Messiah, the Son of the living God.'"[3] Following this same metaphor out I would love to ask those same worship attendees, "But you, what do you say worship is?" Unfortunately, I'm afraid my hopes would fall apart here because I suspect many would respond the same way as the way others see worship, in very shallow ways. This perspective of what worship is is at the core of why I believe so few people make worship a priority in their lives because it has become little more than a burden to them.

I have come to have an entirely different perspective on worship which has completely changed my feelings about the worship experience. Years ago, I freely confess, I too saw worship in much the same way as many people do today: an obligation, something I must do to please God, etc. Over time, especially through my discernment to the call to ordained ministry and the seminary process, I discovered worship is so much more. Worship is not as much about what we do for God; it is much more about what God does for us and allows us to be part of.

Humans are relational creatures. In other words, we exist to be in relationship with others. The others may be our spouse and children, our parents or other relatives, our co-workers or friends, nature, creation, and, yes, even God. This is how we were created, to be in relationship with others. The most basic of human needs proceeding from our created form is to love and be loved, which implies relatedness with God, with others, with creation, and with ourselves.

God created humanity in God's image and likeness.[4] In this formative act in creation, God also formed a relationship with humanity unique to the rest of creation. Although I am processing this from a Christian perspective, this understanding and belief are foundational in Jewish, Muslim, and Christian beliefs. God stated firmly his intent in establishing and maintaining a covenantal relationship with Abram, "I will establish my covenant between me and you, and your offspring after you throughout their generations, for an everlasting covenant, to be God to you and to your offspring after you."[5] From these creative and redemptive foundations, God's intention to be in relationship with humanity has continued throughout the biblical record and time to the present and beyond.

A covenant is not a casual or superficial relationship, but instead, it is a committed relationship where both parties are invested in the relationship without time constraints. The biblical covenants are binding relationships between God and God's people, binding both God and God's people to the relationship. Abram, as previously mentioned, represents one of many of those binding, covenantal relationships and the covenant he enjoyed was marked by the sign of circumcision. Noah's covenant was similar, but marked with the "bow in the clouds."[6] In Christ, we have the New Covenant, marked in Christ's blood establishing the covenant for generations to come.[7] In marriage, we join in a covenantal relationship with our spouse and our sexual intimacy between spouses provides the sign and seal on that covenant. In each case, the covenant is sacred and marked with a sign, establishing a binding relationship without the normal boundaries of time.

The basic relationship with God begins with God. Certainly, this sounds like circular logic, but it isn't. We know God as Father, Son, and Holy Spirit; not three separate beings but God in three persons, yet one God. We often refer to this specifically Christian belief and understanding as to the Holy Trinity or the Triune God. There are many occasions throughout the Gospels of Jesus referring to the Father and to the Spirit in relationship to himself. Most scholars would agree the Gospel of John is most prolific in proclaiming this relationship of the four canonical Gospels.

What transpires between the Father and the Son is nothing short of love and adoration. Jesus says this explicitly, "The Father loves the Son and has placed all things in his hands."[8] Also, "but I do as the Father has commanded me, so that the world may know that I love the Father."[9] The obedience of the Son to the Father and the sending of the Son on behalf of the Father demonstrate a level of love, which is in many ways, beyond our human comprehension. This is a mutual love for one another and for creation. Jesus captures this as, "[no] one has greater love than this, to lay down one's life for one's friends."[10] The love, as Jesus expressed here, I believe is not limited to love for his friends, but also his Father to whom he repeatedly deferred. It was his deep love for both the Father and humanity that propelled Jesus to be willing to lay down his life.

The Nicene Creed along with the Apostles' Creed are two of the foundational creedal statements of belief within the Christian faith. They both, in their own way, profess the basics of belief concerning the Father, the Son, and the Holy Spirit. In the version of the Nicene Creed as used by Christianity in the West, the 3rd article concerning the Holy Spirit says, "[We believe] in the Holy Spirit, the Lord, the life-giver, who proceeds from the Father and the Son, who with the Father and the Son is worshipped and glorified, who has spoken through the prophets."[11] Although there is a 1000-year-old controversy between the Eastern Church and the Western Church concerning the statement "and the Son"[12], there still stands the common belief that the Holy Spirit proceeds from the Father and is worshipped and glorified mutually with the Son.

The Holy Spirit's procession flows out through the Father's will and the act of creation, along with the Son's redeeming obedience and sacrificial love. In God, the Father, the Son, and the Holy Spirit is contained the perfect love of God for the sake of all creation. It is this procession of the Holy Spirit, proceeding through the Father and the Son that sustains and redeems all of creation. This procession is the very embodiment of love without which life in creation would not be possible.

This communion between the Father, and the Son, and the Holy Spirit is in and of itself the very genesis of worship. It is the first and most perfect form of worship that ever has or ever will exist. This worship is the fullest expression of love by the Father for the Son and the Holy Spirit, by the Son for the Father and the Holy Spirit, and by the Holy Spirit for the Father and the Son. Here worship is perfected as an act of mutual love and adoration. It is in this love the Triune God also created worship. Here, is where God's love begins but also proceeds out to His creation.

The Triune God both loves and adores his creation. This love and adoration for God's creation is not different from the love and adoration existing between Father, Son, and Holy Spirit; in fact, it is the same. In this way, God's worship extends to his creation of which we are part. In other words, God's love and adoration for his creation is an act of worship of his creation. Jesus, the Son, acknowledges this humble status when he said, "For the Son of Man came not to be served but to serve, and to give his life a ransom for many."[13]

The worship existing around the relationship of love and adoration of the Father, Son, and Spirit proceeding out to creation is one we are invited into; not forced, but invited. By the very fact we exist, God's love surrounds and enfolds us. But, God invites us to this mutual love and adoration without forcing his will on us. Instead, God's love is made available to us to share and enjoy. Entering into this loving relationship with God we enter into worship.

When we enter worship of God, with God, and with our fellow believers we should enter with joy and thanksgiving. This is something we are invited to, by God, with joy and thanksgiving

36

because God receives us with joy and thanksgiving, and never are we forced to participate in this worship but allowed to. This is God's choosing since when we are free to worship or free not to worship but choose by our free will to worship, the expression of our worship is a genuine expression of our love for God and God's creation. When it is forced it is not from our heart, and God desires our heart not just our actions.

How we experience this worship is somewhat unique to each of us, as each of us is unique. For most of us, we are known and loved in a variety of ways. For some in our lives, we may be co-workers, colleagues, or friends. For others, we may be parent or child, sibling, spouse, aunt or uncle, niece or nephew, etc. For most of us, we are multiple of these to different people. It would be easy for one person to be a father, while also being a son, while also being an uncle, while also being a co-worker, while also being a spouse. That person would not interact with their co-workers in the same manner as they would their spouse; the physically intimate contact appropriate in marriage is generally not acceptable in the workplace. In the same way, each of us relates to our creator in the way in which we were created.

When we begin to realize worship is the loving relationship with God as begun by God toward us, then the definition of worship broadens beyond our human understanding. As a result, our worship could take nearly an infinite number of forms and styles. It is worship in our prayers. It is worship in our gathering in God's name. It is worship in our proclamation of the gospel and God's story of love for us. It is worship in our sharing of

37

God's sacramental gifts. It is worship in our tears, our joys, our praise, and our sadness. And, it is worship in our blessing of one another in God's name. In each of these, we acknowledge and enter into, intentionally, our covenantal relationship with God and one another, "For where two or three are gathered in my name, I am there among them."[14] Therefore, even in the broadness of that new definition, we find ourselves able to enjoy our worshipful relationship with God at every moment, in every way, with everyone in our lives, in God's name.

Ultimately, I want to encourage us all to broaden our definition of worship to go to many facets of our lives. I want us to experience worship in the gathering of God's people for our typical weekly gathering in congregations around the world, singing hymns, reading scripture, hearing proclamation in sermons, and gathering around font and table. However, I also want us to see the other parts of our lives as opportunities for worship as well, and not see worship in such narrow and shallow terms. See our opportunity for worship in choir practice as we harmonize the songs of faith, in songs of praise on our car radios as we travel, in our marriage beds with our dearest earthly companion, in the supermarket greeting our neighbor in the peace of Christ, and in school as we practice forgiveness and reconciliation with classmates. Worship of and with God is too great to limit to one reluctant hour per week as God is too great to be placed in some narrow and confining box.

In the clinical world of pastoral care, our encounters with patients, families, prisoners, staff, and others are also occasions where our time spent could also be seen as times of worship. The call of the clinical pastoral caregiver, or chaplain, is unique, and often, in those settings, times for organized worship for many for whom we care is simply not a realistic possibility. By our mere presence as the chaplain, we bring worship to them, as "two or three are gathered," in the name of God. Together we, patient and chaplain, "pay divine honors to; adore (God),"[15] in that sacred time together.

Without realizing it at the time, I felt the sense of this type of call to bring worship to one who could not experience it in my grandmother long before I decided to respond to a call to ordained ministry. My grandmother's health had declined rapidly over the previous year to the point she struggled to attend worship services, and then eventually could not even do that; the impact was devastating to her. I proposed to my family to find a way to "bring worship to her," and they concurred. Although she died before we could bring this to fruition it was still a moment of transformation for me and my understanding of worship. Worship was indeed possible outside the brick and mortar walls of a traditional church building. Instead, it became possible wherever God's people may gather, and in whatever setting they may be.

God's people gather in the emergency room for broken arms and heart attacks. God's people gather in labor and delivery to welcome newborns and to mourn the unfortunate reality of fetal demises. God's people gather for routine medical exams and the sad realization that a life expectancy is way too short. God's

39

people gather to process the ramifications of a violent assault and to confess the sins that put them in confinement. In these and many other circumstances chaplains, pastors, and other pastoral caregivers have the opportunity to see their encounter as an encounter for worship, or they can view it as simply another aspect of their job. If I could implore anything it would be to encourage these care providers to see their encounters as worship, a moment of something sacred where God is worshipped and adored. It is so much more than just being present or counseling, it is the gathering of God's people in God's name. Acknowledging it as worship acknowledges the mutual relationship with God that brought you together, to begin with, and to experience God's all-embracing love as God extends the worship to and through you.

A helpful reminder to the pastoral caregiver or chaplain is the fact you were called to this sacred calling of caring for God's people. God called the prophets, Moses, Elijah, the Apostles, and you. Each of these and many others were called to a sacred mission and calling to help, in one way or another, to draw God's people closer to God. You are that conduit through whom God will often call and gather his people. You provide that opportunity for God's love to be expressed to his people. And, like it or not, you often will represent the holy and sacred on behalf of God for God's people to express their thanks and praise, their hurts and woes, and whatever other things they wish to lay before their creator.

When the chaplain can begin to see this time spent with those for whom we care as sacred and holy time then it is much easier for the chaplain to invite God's people into a time of worship along with you. Then, even as only two, a congregation has formed and worship has commenced, and something holy unto the Lord has commenced.

What is Liturgy?

Within the Christian worshipping world, there are many things that divide us. It may be our approach to sacramental functions like Holy Baptism and Holy Communion. It may be our beliefs surrounding women in ministry. It may be our stance on sexuality or other controversial issues. No matter what, however, there are certain things as Christians we are absolutely in agreement on.

First, we agree Jesus is the Son of God and Jesus really lived, really died, really rose from the dead, really ascended back to the Father, and he really will return in glory one day. Although this sounds fairly rigid, it is not; there is plenty of room for interpretation about many of these things as Christians we believe concerning Jesus.

Second, whether we refer to baptism in sacramental terms or not, we genuinely agree it is of central importance with what it means to be a Christian. We differ greatly on how we practice it, our theology surrounding it, when to conduct it, where to conduct it, who conducts it, etc. However, across the Christian world we are in concurrence that baptism is central to becoming a disciple of Jesus Christ; even if our understanding of discipleship may vary some.

Third, as Christians, we are all in agreement worship is central to our faith. Worship occurs in myriad ways and myriad settings. Seemingly, new ways to experience and participate in worship arise every day. Worship varies wildly from extreme formality to extreme informality. Some worship includes no music or musical instruments, while others seem to contain nothing but music. This makes me wonder how Martin Luther would have edited his Small Catechism for the inclusion of the possibility of live streaming of a worship service via the internet so members of a congregation could participate from the comfort their living rooms in their pajamas with no human interaction. Nevertheless, no matter how we envision worship, practice worship, or even understand it, all of Christianity would agree on the fact that to participate in worship services of some form is a central tenet across Christianity.

For most, worship is a corporate event where we gather with other believers, but for many, it is entirely a solo event. Worship may be something primarily led by a pastor or priest the congregation observes, or it may be something that is a mutual experience between the congregation and worship leaders.

One of the big divides across the Christian world surrounds the topic discussed in this chapter, liturgy. The origin of the word liturgy comes from Koine or ancient Greek (Greek: λειτουργία), leitourgia, which literally means "work of the people." In its original context, it related to wealthy Greeks helping to support the Greek people and the state. Its modern connotation focuses more on what happens in typical Christian worship as the "work of the church," in praising and worshipping God. In more modern times, liturgy or liturgical refers to a specific style of worship.

Liturgical worship today is taken to be more formal or structured in nature. In an overly broad interpretation, most liturgical churches are typically seen as the "baby baptizing" ones, or ones that would practice infant baptism. The other demarcation you often find in the Christian world is liturgical churches are the ones that practice structured and more frequent celebration of Holy Communion. A third defining factor of many churches typically referred to as liturgical is they typically incorporate the use of one of the various creeds of the church (i.e. Apostles', Nicene, or Athanasian) as a regular part of their worship practices. As a result of these definitions, the Christian world has effectively divided into Liturgical vs. Non-Liturgical. I would counter, however, all Christian worship has a liturgy to it – even if we do not call it as such.

The liturgy, in its simplest form, is our order of worship. The liturgy contains our confessions, our creeds, our calls to worship, our sacramental rites, sermons, prayers, etc. It does not matter if the order of service is primarily clergy-led or if the congregation and clergy do so together. It does not matter what the order is, or if it is the same at every gathering. Whether the congregation is a Catholic congregation using the Latin mass in Rome, or a Pentecostal congregation speaking in tongues in rural North Carolina, a liturgy still exists. An order of worship that each congregation is comfortable with is present and used, and congregations know and expect at least some variation of that normal order of service, or liturgy, to be used each time they gather; it is the norm they expect.

Referring to what happens in any given congregation or gathering of God's people as a liturgy does not imply a particular theology or adherence to a larger church body. The liturgy is just the language of that particular house of worship, or how that congregation relates to God and one another in a time set aside to be sacred and holy.

Every home has its language and patterns. Every couple has their unique love language, which may or may not even be spoken. Every congregation or house of worship has its own language and patterns for worship enabling them to relate to God and one another in the way God created them. That pattern, that language, that order of things is how that congregation worships, how that congregation conveys love to one another and God. The resulting dialogue of love – spoken or not – is their liturgy. And, even if we classify ourselves as "non-liturgical", we still have a liturgy to our worship that is ours.

Every pastor, chaplain, priest, deacon, etc. who provides pastoral care to another person has a pattern they follow which is comfortable and effective for their ministry as well. The reason is simple; as humans, we are habitual creatures, and readily fall into patterns even if we do not intend to. Over the years, I noticed this about myself in my application of pastoral care in hospital settings, or counseling, or prison visits, or any number of other functions fall under my role as a pastor or chaplain.

For example, when making hospital visits, I noticed I have a few different ways of initiating the visit, a period of sharing and discussing, a period of something sacred, and a time to move on. Never were any two visits exactly the same; even if it was to the same person with the same concerns. This is because each person, situation, and time is unique. However, the basic pattern remained. What I unexpectedly discovered was a liturgy to my practice and application of pastoral care.

As the pastoral care provider, I have found comfort in the consistency in relating to the people for whom I care. To reinvent the wheel for every single visit is more challenging than I care to tackle, and frankly not necessary. However, even in the consistency of the pattern of our visits there exists room for spontaneity, exploring new issues, concerns, or praises, there is time for prayer, anointing, or communion, and there is always space to share what God is doing in our lives.

As a Lutheran pastor and chaplain, I resonate well with the four main parts of any worship service which form the skeleton of our worship. Those four main parts are Gathering, Word, Meal, and Sending. In the coming chapters, I plan on discussing each of these in how they appear in a typical worship service, but also how they appear in a pastoral care setting.

When we begin to recognize the patterns of our lives, we begin to see the liturgy that exists in ordinary things; and that is not a bad thing. I have a "liturgy" of preparing for bed, of mowing the grass, of enjoying a meal with my family, etc. My suspicion is each of us has the same, even if we flatly deny our comfort and consistency in how we go about various aspects of our lives because we don't want to be seen as stale or predictable. I encourage us to look beyond that discomfort, however, to the possibility of something sacred being able to happen in the ordinary.

Serving as a chaplain in the Navy I have long experienced watching Sailors practice necessary skills to keep a ship afloat or fight a fire. They know where their damage control equipment is and how to use it because they have practiced using it many, many times. For them, that knowledge and consistency can save their ship and their lives.

Doctors, policemen, engineers, and many others do the same. Each of us has patterns that turn a chaotic situation into one more predictable and manageable. Yet, we leave room in that pattern for the newness and the variations; in this, we creatively adapt to our environment and surroundings.

Our liturgy in terms of our faith life daily will certainly take many forms. For instance, a prayer at mealtimes for most families will begin to take on a form of its own in words and/or form. The words may be something like the familiar, "God is great, God is good…" mealtime prayer or it may be a free-form prayer. It may be with heads bowed and hands joined together, or looking up to heaven with hands raised. Even something as simple as a mealtime prayer will have a liturgy to it, which provides comfort and familiarity to those who make it part of their own.

It is worthwhile to recognize and connect with the liturgies of our everyday lives. In her book, Liturgy of the Ordinary: Sacred Practices in Everyday Life,[1] Tish Harrison Warren explores in beautiful ways how to begin to see the sacred amid our ordinary lives. Essentially, the goal is not to see the sacred and secular divide in our lives so stark, but to see the whole of our lives as sacred. When we begin to see the fullness of our lives, especially the ordinary and mundane parts as Warren does in making her bed, it will change us in ways that allow us to connect more deeply and more spiritually with our creator who does not separate himself from us at any time. Instead, as we conduct the liturgy of making our bed, or making a cup of coffee, or changing our child's dirty diaper as a moment that is sacred and worthy of worship, connecting us with our God who created us and redeems us.

The Gathering

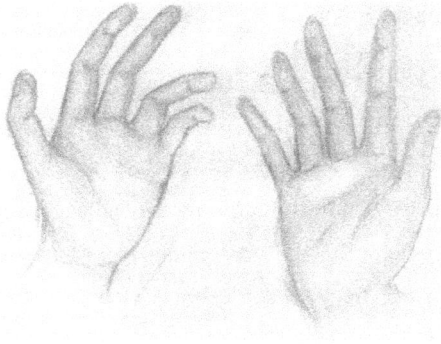

As common sense as it may sound, there is no unimportant part of the liturgy of our worship. Every component of the liturgy is specifically there to engage the congregation in the fullest expression of worship of God, and to experience the mutual presence of God in our midst. Some congregations, pastors, or individuals may place a greater emphasis on one part over another; like the Eucharist or the sermon. However, I want to stress the importance of every element of worship. I am addressing them here in the order in which I am accustomed to them, but I encourage all to consider each element in their own format and language.

There is a great encounter between Moses and the Lord in Exodus 3:11-15. In that encounter, the Lord is calling Moses to serve him by leading his people from Egypt and slavery to freedom and the Promised Land. Moses, understandably, struggles with his worthiness to take on such a task, "Who am I that I should go to Pharaoh, and bring the Israelites out of Egypt?"[1] Moses also struggles with convincing the Children of Israel to follow a God whom they do not fully know, "If I come to the Israelites and say to them, 'The God of your ancestors has sent me to you,' and they ask me, 'What is his name?' what shall I say to them?"[2] At this point, the Lord responds to Moses' concerns and shares his holy name with Moses, "God said to Moses, 'I AM WHO I AM.' He said further, 'Thus you shall say to the Israelites, 'I AM has sent me to you.'"[3]

In the Prophet Isaiah's call, the encounter between him and the Lord is equally compelling. "And [Isaiah] said: 'Woe is me! I am lost, for I am a man of unclean lips, and I live among a people of unclean lips; yet my eyes have seen the King, the Lord of hosts!' Then one of the seraphs flew to me, holding a live coal that had been taken from the altar with a pair of tongs. The seraph touched my mouth with it and said: 'Now that this has touched your lips, your guilt has departed and your sin is blotted out.'"[4]

In both the passage relating to the Lord's call of Moses and the other of Isaiah's call, they are typical of what would be found in the gathering portion in a worship liturgy; greeting one another and acknowledging why we have gathered.

One of the important components in the gathering portion of the liturgy is the worship leader's greeting the congregation and the congregation greeting the worship leader in return. This can be as formal of a greeting as, "The grace of our Lord Jesus Christ, the love of God and the communion of the Holy Spirit be with you all," with a response of, "And also with you," as typical of more formal church settings. Or the greeting can be as informal as, "Good morning, Church," with a reply of "Good morning, Preacher." In every worship service I have ever been part of, in any Christian or even non-Christian tradition, there is some element of greeting as the congregation gathers for worship. However, the same thing occurs visiting your neighbor. As you are welcomed into their home with warmth and friendly compassion greetings are shared common to your relationship and connect with the two of you; it is the liturgical gathering of your friendship. This could be a simple, "Hello", or may include hugs and handshakes. The beautiful thing is, each community and each relationship gets to determine what a greeting will look like, but we all have them.

The greeting in worship is consistent with Moses effectively asking the Lord, "Who are you?" There is a certain intimacy in worship that is necessary. We want to know who it is we worship and with whom we are worshipping. We greet one another, and exchange names or roles to know who will be doing what during this period of worship. Effectively the clergy announces to the congregation, "Today I will be your pastor," and the congregation replies, "Today, we will worship God with you." In all honesty, I have never seen a worship service begin with quite that pedestrian of a greeting, yet, in essence, that is what is occurring in any house of worship; just a little more formal or reverent. But, even that pedestrian of an interchange would work.

Most of us have had or still have the experience of a significant other in our lives. This may be a spouse, a boyfriend/girlfriend, or fiancé. No matter who that person is, there is always a greeting of some form whenever we encounter each other. I cannot imagine coming home from work and not greeting my wife with a hug and kiss, any more than I can imagine not doing so as we begin each day waking up next to each other. This is a sacred part of our relationship. The greeting in other romantic relationships also may be a kiss or a hug, but it is still a very intimate encounter between the two that is, at a certain level, very sacred for that relationship. However, when you first met your significant other and were establishing your relationship, that first greeting also included the same question as Moses had for the Lord, "Who are you?"

The sharing of a name in greeting carries with it a certain implied intimacy and familiarity. It takes even the most casual relationship to another level where more is shared and discussed. The person on the other side of the equation is now no longer a stranger; I know their name. There is a significant power and vulnerability in a name and knowing another person's name. In sharing your name with another you make yourself vulnerable to them and expose a part of yourself you reserve only for the most important relationships in your life.

When you put sharing a name in the context of today's environment, it is on par with sharing your Personally Identifiable Information (PII). A typical person is very cautious about whom they would be willing to share their Social Security Number, date of birth, mother's maiden name, etc. with, and for good reason. Less honest people tend to misuse our private information. Sharing our name requires an implied trust; God's relationship with us is no different.

God gave his holy name, as previously mentioned, to Moses then later placed limitations on how that was to be used. "You shall not make wrongful use of the name of the Lord your God, for the Lord will not acquit anyone who misuses his name."[5] Convey the same dignity and respect to our earthly relationships; do not misuse the gift of the name and implied intimacy that has been shared with us by anyone.

At the beginning of a worship relationship between God and God's people, or even between God's people, we make ourselves vulnerable. We share who we are. But, God does the same thing for us in sharing with us he is the "Great I AM." It is an intimate bond between us, that God has chosen to expose part of who he is to us and allow us to see behind that portion of the veil that could separate us. Instead, the veil is pulled aside for us to glimpse upon God's greatness. In this, even the Great I AM has made himself vulnerable to us in our times of worship.

Whenever I encounter someone in a pastoral care relationship, whether in a hospital room, my office, the chapel, or even in prison, the first task is always to greet one another. We introduce ourselves to one another, and by doing so, we establish boundaries and expectations. Even if we have met on numerous occasions we still take the opportunity for a polite greeting that re-establishes why we are gathering on that particular occasion.

Frequently, a Sailor will enter my office with one concern or another. At the point they cross my threshold, I rarely have any idea of what their concern may be, and in many circumstances, I have never met them before. For me, the gathering portion of this liturgical dance began before they ever walked through my door. Whether they would ever admit it or not, I am convinced that God's Holy Spirit rested on them, giving them the courage to seek a potential path to healing and hope. For this reason, I do not turn people away but instead, strive with all my being to meet them with the belief God has orchestrated this encounter believing the setting for worship to exist was set by God. For at that moment, I cannot be convinced the person I am greeting at my door is any different from the strangers Abraham met only to discover he had hosted God.[6]

My goal at that moment is to set a table that is welcoming and inviting, with no expectations on them; the expectations are on me. I want my "guest" to feel they have found a place of peace amid the chaos of their life. To do this, I greet them personally and usher them to a comfortable chair. I always have tissues available because I never know if the conversation will be one of tears, joy, or both. Frequently, they enter my office upset and struggling with some challenge or dilemma that is, as of yet, unspoken. At that moment, it is not uncommon for them to begin our conversation, before I ever have a chance to speak, with, "I don't even know where to begin."

That opening is one I have heard more times than I can count, and I am quite sure I will hear it many more. Even in that seemingly meaningless opening, it gives me a clue about the depth of the anguish they are facing. However, to complete the liturgy of greeting and establish the atmosphere that defines why we are there, and the boundaries and expectations of our relationship, I take the lead and offer, "Well, let's start with the easy stuff," as I extend my hand to shake theirs, "I am Chaplain Connolly." At that moment I see them begin to relax and I continue, "Why don't you tell me a little about yourself." I further encourage them to not only share their last name or their rank but also their first name, which often really surprises them. I do this intentionally because, especially in a military environment, even casual interactions can feel very impersonal; I want their encounter with me to feel personal and meaningful.

In this moment of mutual vulnerability, my guest was welcomed, invited to take a seat of honor, and offered a safe place to open this time of worship. I have intentionally shared with them at that moment not so much my position of authority, but my position of service to them. As their chaplain or pastor, they now know what my responsibility is to them, and my role in caring for them. I do frequently have to remind, especially junior personnel, my rank should not be seen as a barrier, but as a tool available to them to help them open the doors they need. I do often have the access they do not have because of my rank, and that is there to help them. My role as their chaplain is to be their servant; they are in charge.

For the next few minutes, I gently encourage my guests to share more about themselves with me. I intentionally try to steer away from the "ugly situation" that may have encouraged them to seek me out for a moment to establish trust and rapport. I encourage them to share with me about them as a person, not a rank or a job, but a person. I want to know who they are and where they are from. I guide my questions and conversation to hear more about the individual with whom I now share my space. Pastoral care encounters are so personal and so intimate, and it is my responsibility as their chaplain to make this a safe and welcoming encounter.

In the Lutheran tradition, as we continue the gathering portion of our worship, we quickly come to a point of corporate confession and absolution. In the corporate form of our confession, it is broad and all-encompassing. However, Lutherans, as do our Catholic and Episcopal siblings and so many others, also include as part of our offering private confession. In the private setting our confessions are no longer general, but take a specific form of that which grieves us personally. The pastor, priest, or chaplain is also quite free to adopt words that liberate a person to freely share their confession and equally free to proclaim an absolution that is targeted and specific.

In many ways, the confession is why we gather to worship a crucified and risen savior, to begin with. Apart from our sin, we have no need for Jesus. Yet, we are sinful and have been so since the fall of humanity recorded in Genesis 3. Stating this here does not imply, however, we believe we are sinful; at least not universally. Until we acknowledge the reality of sin in our lives and our world we remain powerless to doing anything about the sin that pervades our very existence. When we acknowledge our sin, the brokenness around us, and our powerlessness to do anything about it we then are prepared to receive the grace of what only Jesus can do for us: forgive us and heal us. It is in that moment we come to the realization we are not, never have been, nor ever will be God; only God is God. Our lot in life is to be the creation God made good, but we have not always executed our role as good. In fact, we have consistently chosen sin for our path no matter how noble our intentions may be. Thus, we need what only Jesus brings, forgiveness.

Very soon after a guest arrives in my office or I arrive in their space, he or she will begin to weave into their story of who they are why they have sought me out; the "ugly situation" alluded to earlier. Often this takes the form of anger, grief, pain, lament, shame, or any of many other things that weigh them down as they pour out their concerns of what has occurred to them or of which they have done and are ashamed. This moment is one of the most vulnerable in our entire encounter, and the moment where the greatest dignity and respect for my guest is called for. No matter what they may choose to share it is my responsibility to receive it as a sacred offering and recognition they are powerless over the presence of sin in their lives; even if they are the very source of their sin.

This sharing of their story is the sharing of their confession. It may or may not be as formal as the typical opening in the Sacrament of Reconciliation our brothers and sisters in the Roman Catholic Church use, "Bless me, Father, for I have sinned," but it

57

is equally palpable. Sin has entered their life, and they, at a minimum, need to discuss this and unload it. The burden of the reality of this sin is too great to carry alone, so those who seek us out as their clergy are seeking us out to help carry their burden.

An important note here, we are called to help carry their burden, not lay more on them. When our responses to their confession cast more blame on them, or are hurtful in other ways, we heap on more of a burden instead of relieving the burden they already carry.

Jesus proclaimed, "Come to me, all you that are weary and are carrying heavy burdens, and I will give you rest. Take my yoke upon you, and learn from me; for I am gentle and humble in heart, and you will find rest for your souls. For my yoke is easy, and my burden is light."[7] At some point in the DNA of those who seek us out as their clergy, I believe this promise of Jesus is swirling around in them, and I believe the Holy Spirit is the one swirling it around. They know they are carrying a heavy burden and they know there is a place they can find rest, even if they do not know or even believe God in Christ Jesus is the one who offers that rest. However, they do know it is a spiritual concern and the chaplain's office is the place to address spiritual concerns; therefore they seek out the chaplain.

Constantly I reflect on my ordination vows as they continue to guide my ministry. I am not, nor do I pretend to be Jesus. However, addressing those who are heavy burdened is just as much my ministry as it was for Jesus. The last of my ordination vows reminds me of that fact, "Will you give faithful witness in the world, that God's love may be known in all that you do?"[8] Fulfilling this vow does not mean to chastise, berate, belittle, laugh at, or any number of other things that can be equally cruel. Instead, fulfilling this vow means receiving what is offered in love, that God's love may be known. Fulfilling this vow is the courage to mourn and grieve with them as this confession of the sinfulness of life and the world is shared; not lord my superiority over them, but to come down with them into the valley as a fellow sinner on this pilgrimage of life.

It is a long-held tradition and belief of many Christian traditions the pastor or priest is entrusted with the "keys to the kingdom" to either retain or forgive sins. This tradition traces its roots to Peter's confession of who Jesus is from which Jesus established the church and the office of the pastor along with the expectations of the pastor.[9] Although I do struggle with having that kind of power and authority entrusted to one such as myself, I do take the role seriously. I have been entrusted with the weighty responsibility of proclaiming either forgiveness of sins confessed, or with retaining those same sins.

In total transparency, I have yet to refuse anyone who has come to me and bared their sins and their soul for me to see. The reason for this is I can never possibly know the true depth of their contrition at the moment. What I have in front of me to work with is one who was concerned enough to confess their wrongs, which in itself requires tremendous vulnerability on their part. The person is required to admit to their wrongs and their shames. I do not see my job or role at that point to further condemn them but to serve in much the same capacity as did Jesus.

Many wrongs or sins that are committed have earthly consequences over which I have zero control or authority. My guest may have stolen, lied, committed adultery, or any number of other grievous sins. My position is to stand with them in their relationship with God and help restore that relationship through confession and forgiveness. I firmly believe in doing this and have witnessed this fact, that when their relationship with God is restored the individual is at a much greater place of peace to deal with the earthly consequences of their sinful behavior. If I withhold that forgiveness then the individual is neither reconciled with the world or God, and they become hopeless. But, when at least the relationship with God is restored then hope still exists.

In the Gospel of John, Jesus encountered a woman caught in the act of adultery. The legalistic crowd sought to have her stoned to death, which was technically the appropriate punishment for that particular sin.[10] Jesus, however, never said or indicated she had not sinned, but he did not condemn her. Instead, Jesus extended God's grace and mercy and encouraged her to go on her way, freed from the sin of her past and to sin no more.[11] The text does not indicate the depth of the woman's contrition, only her guilt. It mentions nothing about her even seeking Jesus' forgiveness or a "second chance." What the text does demonstrate, however, is the depth of God's grace as manifested in Christ Jesus.

When I use this passage from John as a lens to guide my willingness to proclaim forgiveness to one who has come to me with issues of the sins of the world weighing them down my inclination is to forgive them all and let God sort them out. I cannot possibly know the depth of their contrition or genuineness, but I do know they have come seeking to find one to help them carry the burden; I am such a one. I will proclaim forgiveness freely even if I find it personally challenging or repugnant because if for no other reason, they have made the leap of faith to seek it. My insecurities or human failings should never impede another's spiritual growth and healing.

The forgiveness may be openly spoken if that is what the person is seeking. However, most often I simply receive their story, but with the same sanctity as if they were seeking forgiveness. I do not laugh at, ridicule, or belittle them because of their foolishness or sinfulness. Instead, I receive their story, their lament, and their concern with love. That act of gracious and faithful receiving is an act of forgiveness and reconciliation before I ever open my mouth.

One caution in the proclamation of forgiveness is to not be too quick to pronounce that forgiveness or absolution. For this reason, I want the individual to guide me. If I pronounce forgiveness before they are ready or desiring to receive it, they will not receive what I offer with the grace and mercy intended. Instead, they could view me as flippant of their struggle. Some, in fact many, may need for the ugliness of their sin to invade our space for a while before we simply dispense with it out of hand.

If I listen, truly listen, to their confession I get a better idea of what they need at that moment. However, it is also quite appropriate to explicitly ask what they desire from you as their chaplain at that moment. In paying attention to what they are asking for and needing you meet their pastoral care needs in a much more compassionate way. In many ways, this was the whole premise in George Bennett's book, <u>When They Ask for Bread</u>[12], and I highly recommend it to all who embark on pastoral care ministry.

An example that may amplify the scenario of not jumping too quickly to grant absolution would be situations of moral injury. Moral injury is a situation in which an individual has either done or failed to do something that compromised their core beliefs, values, or virtues. Often, the individual would not take your proclamation of absolution seriously if it is given too quickly because it is too much of a leap for them to believe that God or anyone would be able to forgive their particular sin. Those of us who are pastoral care providers certainly understand that this is not very solid theology on their part to limit what God can or cannot do, but theological debates are not what an individual suffering from a moral injury is seeking. They may need to "confess" their "sins" many times before they are prepared to hear that they are forgiven. Allow them to guide you so that you will be sensitive to what they want and need, and not perceived as some flippant pastor who just wants to put an unwanted check in the box; they will let you know when they are ready.

In a typical congregation, we gather weekly, or even more frequently for organized worship opportunities. We repeat this process of gathering, and this liturgy every time we gather. In a pastoral care environment, such as a hospital or a chaplain's office or prison, we may repeat this process frequently or this may be a single time occurrence. No matter how often, if ever, we repeat the gathering, it sets the tone for the balance of the encounter. The gathering should be just as sacred of an encounter the one-hundredth time as it is the first time. As the clergy, we are the gracious host, welcoming in love and compassion any whom we encounter, receiving their offering of themselves to the encounter as an act of faith, trust and love.

So, what does all this have to do with us as pastoral caregivers? The short answer would be a lot. The lot, however, is not so much changing what we do, but instead, change how we perceive it. When we greet a person on a pastoral care visit in their hospital room no longer look at it as fulfilling some obligation as a chaplain so it can be documented in their charts they received the obligatory pastoral care visit. Instead, shift our focus to the opening strains of a symphony of worship you are initiating with that person. Shift your view from clinical hours to a sacred period of *chronos* or God's time. You are greeting them and gathering with them for a time of worship, and it is not simply their time of worship but yours as well.

The second thing that should be affected by this mindset is the liturgy you use. As I mentioned previously, this does not have to be formal, but it should be intimate, appropriate, and sacred.

63

You are expressing the first few lines of a time of worship, and the words you choose can help whoever you have come to visit see it that way or see it as you simply putting a check in the box. As God the Father, Son, and Spirit invite and enjoy a mystical time of worship which we are invited into as love, we too invite those for whom we care into a time of worship along with us to worship the God who created and forgives us.

Finally, remember you are part of the worship experience. If the pastor standing in front of a congregation is absent from the worship experience the congregation knows and it sours the experience for all. If the chaplain standing in a hospital room is absent from whomever they have come to visit it is equally a dissatisfying experience for the person in the hospital bed. Be present, and worship the God whom you have come to represent and called you into this ministry. Enter the time of worship, fully in your heart. With your heart fully present the words of your liturgy of gathering will take care of themselves.

Other Gathering practices to consider:

1.   Knock and request permission to come in before you enter. Few things sour an encounter like walking in on a patient or other individual when they are in a compromising position, like on the toilet or dressing. This is your first act of dignity and respect.

2.   Check with the nurses' station, or the equivalent in other settings, before attempting a visit. Many patients, for instance, may require protective clothing, gloves, and masks on your part before entering. This simple step

also prevents walking in when a patient is in a compromising position.

3. In a clinical setting where you are initiating the visit inform yourself in advance of their medical, legal, or other situation. This is not to "pollute" the encounter with your knowledge, but to allow you to be sensitive to what concerns may exist.

4. Prepare your staff. Your staff often give the first impression of what someone may encounter with you before you ever have a chance. If they are not gracious, welcoming, and protective then your encounter with the individual will not be as effective or healing because of the deficit you are starting with.

5. For situations where you have "walk-ins" spend time preparing your space in advance. Keep it clean, inviting, and welcoming. Anticipate needs such as tissue, temperature, and privacy. However, also consider their and your safety. I prefer even a small window in my door so that all can be seen even if they cannot be heard.

6. Anticipate various pastoral care concerns for which you may want documentation, referral resources, scripture, etc. I, for example, tend to keep readily printed out a liturgy for individual confession available in my office, as well as oil for anointing and Bibles. I also have printed out information on various other helping agencies we typically refer to so that I do not have to interrupt the encounter to seek it out.

7. Don't forget to pray. Before you walk in their room or enter their space, pray. This is the invocation of your worship service, and it begins with you, the clergy. Invoke God's presence and seek God's gifts for the ministry you are about to embark on.

The Word

The word is not simply a biblical pronouncement. It is also too simple, although correct, to say THE word is Jesus. The word is beyond our scripture, beyond our savior, beyond our pronouncement, and beyond our prayers. The word is all that, and more than our human words will ever fully capture. The word is creative and redeeming, comforting and correcting, living among us and living beyond us. For us, on a human plane, however, it is easiest for us to begin to capture the essence of the word as found in our sacred scriptures, the Bible.

The biblical record documents God's holy history with his people. It records the beautiful bits and the not so beautiful parts. The Bible is incredibly transparent as to the foolishness of God's people and the ever-present faithfulness of God. In the first three chapters of Genesis alone we witness God creating the world in love, humanity introducing a divide between humankind and God through sin, humanity suffering the reality of death because of sin, and God making the first sacrifice to cover the humans' shame. That same pattern is repeated throughout the Bible, and although humanity finds new and creative ways to sin God continues to provide for, care for, and redeem humanity. Humanity certainly has suffered throughout this history for its misdeeds, but the greatest suffering was borne by God.

From a Christian perspective, the closest in time to our present existence are the 27 books comprising the New Testament from approximately 2000 years ago. For our Jewish brothers and sisters, one needs to travel back in time yet another 400 years or more. Yet, contained in these pages this biblical story continues to speak truths to us today that are pertinent to our current reality.

Reading, singing, intoning, praying, and meditating using sacred scripture is integral to worship. Most congregations have particular ways they go about incorporating the sacred scriptures into their worship experience that may include several of the ways mentioned previously or others unique to them; this is not a one size fits all situation. Including scripture directly into our worship experience is a liturgical element of our worship. We may choose to use a certain translation, or use a specific introduction, or even how scripture is included. For instance, the Psalms are often sung, intoned, or read responsively. No matter how it is done, it is easy to see a pattern develop in each house of worship.

Each week, pastors, rabbis, and priests scour these sacred writings looking for the "כה אמר יהוה"[1] ("Thus says the Lord") that speaks to the congregation they shepherd. They each painstakingly seek the truth of what God is saying through them to their congregation, while also listening for God's still small voice to them. For clergy who regularly preach on sacred scripture this is their goal, to connect the biblical truths to the flock with whom they have been entrusted in such a way that it applies to their congregation's current situation in life, while still being faithful to the original intent and focus of the biblical text. This is not always a very easy, or even a very pleasant task. But, this is the task and calling of any clergy. This proclamation is often pivotal to what many have come to associate with a properly conducted worship service, and thus the sermon is a liturgical lynchpin to worship.

Incorporated into the word portion of our worship is woven in what we believe. What we believe inhabits our prayers and relationship with one another. In that way, we pray to God on behalf of the world, our congregation, our community, or the concerns on our hearts. How we pray may have a structure to it or it may be completely unstructured and freeform. It may be solely led by the clergy or an appointed worship assistant, or it may be led by various members of the congregation. No matter what, our prayers inhabit our worship.

What we believe is the very foundation of our life in faith. For many congregations, our beliefs are codified in sharing a common creedal statement like the Apostles' Creed, the Nicene Creed, or others. Other congregations do not practice this, but just because it is not formalized as part of their corporate worship does not mean that the congregation does not have a common belief, consistent throughout their body. Most members of a given congregation can relatively easily share with you, formalized or not, a basic statement and understanding of their belief in who they are, who God is, and how they relate to each other; this is their creed.

What does the word portion of worship look like in a pastoral care setting? Is it reading, singing, proclaiming, interpreting, or something else? The reality is it is all the above or whatever may work well in that setting; we are not locked into one pattern. It is the liturgical element we are considering, and it is an important liturgical element, but we are free to choose how we incorporate it into these encounters. I will propose a few options, but I would encourage the pastoral caregiver to explore these and, and many other ways of recognizing or incorporating the word in your pastoral care practice.

When you visit with a person an incredible way to break into this world from a pastoral care perspective is to allow the person to share their favorite biblical text, one they have heard or been studying recently, or one they are curious about. Read the text together and allow the person in the hospital bed to be the preacher, explaining and exploring what that text means to them. Encourage them to share how God is speaking to them through that text, and how it connects with their current reality. You may hear words of hope, words of anger, words of sorrow, or any of several responses.

Of course, turning this control over to the person you are visiting may cause incredible anxiety in the chaplain; we are, of course, accustomed to being the one choosing the text and expounding on it. However, if the chaplain can maintain the discipline to allow the person to do the preaching and the preacher not do it, then the person becomes free to share what they are feeling without being told by some uninformed chaplain how they should be feeling. This can be a genuine exploration of the word informative to the pastoral caregiver, and healing for the person receiving their care; especially if they know their chaplain is truly listening to them. In that way, it may be the first time in their life they have genuinely been heard, and it is the chaplain who is standing in the place of God and hearing on behalf of God one of God's children pouring out their heart. As Elaine Ramshaw points out, "The minister who prays with a person without first listening to her produces a prayer which bears only a chance relationship to her needs."[2] Knowing and acknowledging scriptural needs is just as important.

Another practice that could easily be incorporated into the word portion of our pastoral care liturgy is Lectio Divina. "Literally [translated from the Latin, Lectio Divina] is 'divine reading' and this practice is sometimes referred to as praying the Scriptures. By following a prescribed method, individuals immerse themselves in a particular Scripture. In classic Lectio Divina, there are four steps in this method: Read (*Lectio*), Meditate (*Meditatio*), Pray (*Oratio*), and Contemplate (*Contemplatio*)."[3] The same text would be read through four times with a different focus each time. The first is simply to Read the text and let it resonate with you. The second would be to read the text and then Meditate on it and see where it leads you. The third time is to allow the text to be your Prayer as you read the

71

text aloud. The fourth would be to read the text for a final time and Contemplate how it is speaking to you today, in your current setting.

A chaplain using Lectio Divina with a patient he or she is visiting could approach using this from a variety of ways. The chaplain could read the text himself or herself all four times, alternate between the chaplain reading and the patient reading, allow family and/or hospital staff to read, etc. There is no one right or wrong way. Often, different voices, cadences, translations, etc. can be very helpful in hearing the different ways we speak to and hear from God.

It is increasingly more and more likely a given hospital will have somewhere on its property a prayer labyrinth. A prayer labyrinth is usually a single path, more or less circular, weaving in and out as you follow the path from the outer edge of the labyrinth to the center and then returning to the outer edge. It is intended the person using the prayer labyrinth would meditate on a text, pray, or both. As the penitent journeys to the center of the labyrinth they should come to grips with the reality of the weights upon them, and as they follow the path back out they should gradually turn those concerns over to God.

Although a prayer labyrinth is more of a solitary practice it can be done as a group, as each person conducts their journey. However, as a group, it can be helpful to reflect on and share the nature of their journey to the center of the labyrinth and back out, discussing the weight they bore and the feeling of releasing that weight to God.

Inviting a patient and / or their family members to join you in a prayer labyrinth can be a great opportunity to build a community of faith for healing and hope. Incorporating this into the word of our liturgy of pastoral care could be done by introducing a scripture verse or passage each participant reflects on. It can be done through a common prayer shared and repeated throughout the journey such as Kyrie Eleison (Lord have mercy) or the Lord's Prayer (the Our Father).

The circular, spiraling nature of a prayer labyrinth is not imperative. The more important part is walking the journey of prayer, contemplatively. Most hospitals are constructed in such a way that patients can easily walk the hallways, or roll their wheelchair or gurney through the hallway. Also, many have somewhat of a repetitive path a person could follow. In other words, the hallways could become the labyrinth you and your patients traverse. Using a single hallway, for instance, a person could make a certain number of laps clockwise representing the journey to the center of the labyrinth followed by the same number of laps counter-clockwise representing the journey from the center back to the outer edge of the labyrinth. Creativity and innovation on the part of the chaplain can make this a very successful and meaningful experience for the patient and / or family members for whom they are caring.

Imagine as well, the sense of community and sharing that could occur as one person pushes the wheelchair for another as they traverse the labyrinth. Or, a couple expecting their first child who needs to walk to induce labor anyway walking the labyrinth and sharing their fears and anxieties of parenthood on the way in, and their joys and excitement on the way out. Again, be creative.

Lectio Divina and Prayer Labyrinths are very contemplative practices that are certainly not suited for everyone, and neither is every chaplain prepared to lead this type of spiritual exercise. However, for the right chaplain and patient, this could prove to be a very healing and helpful way of incorporating the word portion of your liturgy of pastoral care. It would be highly recommended in using either of these practices to discuss it thoroughly, in advance. Discuss with the patient what they could experience and what they will not. Also, after either exercise, be sure to discuss with your patient what they gained from the experience of either Lectio Divina or the Prayer Labyrinth. Ideally, that would be a slightly different experience each time they are exposed to this spiritual discipline.

Music has captured the essence of our faith for millennia. Much of the psaltery is attributed to King David who composed and sang the songs of faith three millennia ago. However, approximately 400 years before David came on the scene was Moses with his incredible hymn of thanksgiving and praise following the children of Israel's transit through the sea, escaping the Egyptians.[4] Since the days of Moses and David music has continued to be an expression of our faith whether it is songs of praise, songs of lament, or songs of hope. The vast majority of these songs find their origins in scripture, and in our singing, we are also proclaiming scripture.

Music has a way of connecting with us and our souls in ways simple words alone often fail to do. However, when you connect the words with a tune it resonates in our DNA in a way that becomes even more meaningful and even more unforgettable.

One of my grandfathers, Sam, spent the last few years of his life under the humbling effects of Alzheimer's Disease. It started deceptively and gradually so that our family wasn't universally convinced that anything was wrong. However, the more the disease took hold the more it robbed him of what made him my grandfather. It was unsettling to me when I had to come to the painful reality he did not even remember who I was, his eldest grandchild. However, what brought tears of joy to my eyes was the realization his faith was still part of who he was; he remembered God even when he did not remember me. He remembered God even when he didn't remember who he was himself. How I realized this is when he, along with several residents in the care facility he was in at the time, were able to stand and sing every verse of several hymns from memory even when they could no longer remember their names or take care of many of their most basic needs like bathing and dressing. This is not implying they sang on key or even completely coherently, but they did recognize the hymns of their faith as part of who they were at the most basic of all levels, in their spirit. On days like that, I am convinced it is the Holy Spirit who sings through and for us.

A chaplain who can incorporate the hymns into the caregiving can experience similar levels of connection. An approach would be to invite your patient or family member to share with you their favorite hymn and further explore what causes that particular hymn to connect with them in the way it does. This type of invitation opens doors to a person's faith history, their understanding of who God is, their understanding of who they are in connection with God. As with favorite Bible verses or passages, it provides a window into their soul where you, as their chaplain, are invited to visit and share. In many cases, it would even be appropriate to sing the hymn together.

There is a certain peace that transpires in music that can do much to provide healing and lessen our anxious spirits. King Saul is recorded as having struggled significantly, and at the recommendation of his counsel sought out someone to provide music for the king to help in his most troubled moments. The response was, "[whenever] the evil spirit from God came upon Saul, David took the lyre and played it with his hand, and Saul would be relieved and feel better, and the evil spirit would depart from him."[5] The presence of music was calming.

The creeds, as mentioned previously, are an important element of many congregational worship services. Sharing what we believe, even if our congregation does not use formal creedal statements is consistent with what it means to be a Christian. In this portion of our pastoral care encounter, it would also be quite appropriate to discuss what we believe. Invite the person you are visiting with to simply share with you what it is they believe; who is God to them and how do they understand God. This simple sharing can give a chaplain incredible insight into a person's location on their faith journey and what their sense of hope may or may not look like.

The practices mentioned here are in no way meant to be an exhaustive representation of ways to explore the word portion of our liturgy. Read, pray, meditate, discuss, and sing scripture; this is our experience of the word in our worship and our liturgy of pastoral care. However, as the chaplain you also are part of the gathered worshipers in this experience; don't forget to be part of it and not separate from it.

A caveat to mention in closing for this section, clergy are, in theory, theologically trained and prepared to shepherd whatever flock God has called them to. The same cannot be said for those to whom we offer our pastoral care. When you dare to allow the person you are visiting to share their faith with you or to share their interpretation of scripture, or even to pray, you really must also have the fortitude to hold your tongue. Nitpicking every theological detail with them to ensure that their theology is in alignment with yours is not very helpful or effective in your pastoral care ministry. Life and faith both are a journey, and it is arrogant of us to believe that we have all the answers or that we have it all figured out. Be humble and allow the person you are visiting to openly share. If you cannot figure this out it is very unlikely you would be invited or welcome back the next time.

The Meal

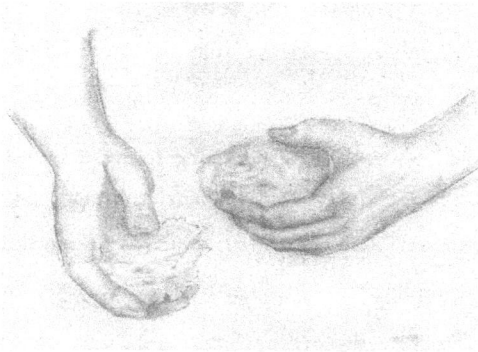

In most homes, there is something sacred about family mealtime. Many homes in 21st Century America struggle to establish any resemblance of family time. However, that last holdout, even if infrequently observed, is the family dinner. All the TVs are turned off. All phones are put away. It is a sacred and holy time, set apart for a family to not only dine together but also share their lives. I do not doubt that I am showing a personal bias here, but I do believe personally it is that important.

Truth in advertising, my own family struggles to keep this practice consistent, but it is a priority we have set and we do all we can to keep this time "sanitized" from the world around us. We pray together, we share a meal, and we discuss our day. The good stuff, the funny stuff, the sad stuff; it all comes out.

I can easily imagine a similar scene with our Lord Jesus Christ some 2,000 years ago as he paused intentionally to share a meal, his last in fact, with his disciples. Twelve apostles, other men and women of the community, and Jesus gathered to celebrate a Passover meal. The meal was a celebration of life resulting from death, and deliverance of the Children of Israel from Pharaoh's oppressive rule. Some 1,400 years later, Jesus and his followers were still celebrating God's deliverance.

The conversation around the table certainly had to do with their faith and their common Jewish heritage, defined through that Exodus event. However, I am equally certain their reality on that evening included its joys, sorrows, successes, and defeats which were on their minds and their tongues. They dined as we dine, with a sacredness to the gathering of God's people.

Now, here we are 3,400 years after the Exodus event and 2,000 years after Jesus celebrated this first Eucharistic meal with his disciples. As the Passover meal continues to connect the Jewish people to God's deliverance so does the Eucharistic meal connect Christians to God's salvation. These meals are more than just symbols to us; they tangibly connect us to our relationship with God, God's deliverance, and God's salvation – past, present, and future. In these meals, we experience hope, as our Jewish brothers and sisters so eloquently and hopefully proclaim after their Seder meal at Passover, "בירושלים הבאה לשנה", or "Next year in Jerusalem."

The Eucharistic meal, or as commonly referred to, Holy Communion, is a very specific part of our typical worship service. The meal is the Eucharist, the Lord's Supper, and in a liturgical worshipping community is celebrated at nearly every gathering.

79

Without delving into divisive theology surrounding Transubstantiation, Consubstantiation, or Memorial Meal in description of this portion of our liturgy it would be sufficient to say this is a center of gravity in our typical Christian worship that is sacred, holy, and set apart where we encounter God in an intimate, tangible, and unique way.

For the more liturgical traditions, this meal is often referred to as a sacrament, which unfortunately even that word is loaded and carries baggage and expectations with it that are inconsistent from one Christian faith group to another. However, for those traditions which use sacramental language this meal is always counted among the sacraments no matter how a sacrament is defined in that tradition or how many sacraments they may observe. Therefore, even if a chaplain may or may not come from a liturgical or even a sacramental tradition there is a fairly universal appreciation and reverence for this meal across the Christian world.

The meal portion of a typical worship service is where the gathered worshippers have the opportunity to participate in, receive, and/or observe something set apart as sacred. The Eucharistic meal is but one of those possibilities which are a means of God's grace being bestowed upon us and shared among us. Traditionally, the means of God's grace are The Triune God, Proclamation of the Word, Holy Baptism, and Holy Communion.[1] However, I would encourage broadening the appreciation of what would be appropriate in this more sacramental portion of a pastoral care visit. Consider ways that God's grace could be extended to the mourning, the sick, the hopeless, and others. Then, consider how the chaplain may preside at such a function as a part of his or her liturgy of pastoral care. I want to offer some specific possibilities here, but I encourage the creative chaplain to not think of these to be an exhaustive representation of what could be offered.

As a prelude to whatever is done during this part of our pastoral care encounter, it is helpful for the chaplain to be in the right mindset with his or her heart properly attuned to what is about to occur. Where the Eucharist is provided in a typical worship service there is a portion before the Eucharistic liturgy begins that is referred to as "setting the table."

Setting the table is exactly what it sounds like whether you are preparing for a family meal at home or preparing to serve Holy Communion to your congregation; what is to be shared is set out, visibly, so all can see and share. How this is done, however, is vitally important.

Setting the table in Holy Communion is setting out and uncovering the bread and the wine so that it is prepared to be served. But, it is not simply set out like some cheap truck stop diner where plates are practically thrown on the table. No, instead all elements are set out with reverence for God, and demonstrating to God's people they also are worth every effort you are putting into setting a table for them.

No matter what the sacramental function may be that is offered at this time, there is a certain "setting the table" portion of it that demonstrates to God's people that both God and they are revered and valued. We have all certainly been to restaurants where we felt like an imposition to the wait staff, and others where the wait staff lovingly cared for our every need. The people of God do not want a chaplain who makes them feel like the communion that is being offered is an imposition to him or that God's people are. Instead, the people of God want a chaplain who offers all their pastoral care efforts with love and care.

First, consider bringing the Eucharistic meal as an extension of God's grace to patients, family members, and staff. Serving in a hospital previously I would frequently provide worship services, but very few of the patients were able to join the services because of their physical limitations. Most staff members were not able to leave the wards they were attending, and many family members chose to stay with their infirmed patient. However, bringing the Eucharist to a patient's room, to a nursing station, or a waiting room proved a powerful connection to those who chose to receive. The joy that was present on their faces as we discussed the text for the day, prayed together and shared the communion liturgy was palpable. Then, placing the elements of Holy Communion in their hands was healing for them as they realized they too were part of the great cloud of witnesses as the Body of Christ in union with one another through that meal.

A wise chaplain, of course, realizes that not every patient can receive the elements of communion or should receive them for health reasons. For instance, if a patient is preparing for surgery or is in some observation mode their medical provider may specify that they are NPO, indicating that they should take neither food nor liquid by mouth until that order is lifted. As life-giving as we believe by faith the Eucharist to be, in a case like this it could prove deadly.

A challenging lesson that I learned in this was to be more mindful of the patients who do request to receive Holy Communion. I had one situation where I was distributing communion to patients, family, and staff. The nursing staff informed me that one of our patients wished to receive communion. As a hospital staff chaplain, it was my responsibility to document the fact that I had provided a sacramental visit to a patient in their charts. As I went to do so for this particular patient I noticed an allergy warning in her charts indicating an allergy to grape juice. Fortunately, the patient was not severely allergic, but neither the patient nor the nursing staff had cautioned me before providing the communion elements to her. As a result, our procedures changed so that nursing staff was required to review for potential allergies before the distribution of communion.

The second great sacrament in the Lutheran church is baptism. It is cleansing. It is welcoming. It is blessing. It is an act of the individual, an act of the church, and an act of God meeting in a sacred moment, extending God's grace to the unclean as an act of sanctification, justification, and salvation. And, as central as this act is to what it means to be a Christian it is amazing to me how divided the Christian world is concerning this cleansing bath.

Christianity cannot agree on who should and should not be baptized. Is it for infants? Is it appropriate only for those able to verbally confess faith? Is it appropriate for the developmentally challenged?

Christianity cannot agree on how it should be conducted. Should it only be conducted as part of corporate worship, or can it be a standalone function apart from the gathered congregation worshiping as a body? Can it be conducted in freshwater or saltwater or either? Must it be conducted by bodily immersing a person or can water be poured over their heads? Must the water be flowing or can it be standing? Must it be conducted only by ordained clergy or can laypersons baptize? Can it be conducted by pouring water from a canteen in the middle of a desert (as has often happened with deployed service members)?

As with Holy Communion, Holy Baptism is central and formative to what it means to be a Christian; on this, the Christian world proclaims with one voice. However, as with Holy Communion, Holy Baptism has its own very divided theology defining it, and each Christian body has labored over how they interpret scripture relating to this most important of sacraments to such a point that each body is very passionate about why the way that they observe this sacrament is correct. I believe that each church body has approached this faithfully, prayerfully, and deliberately to ensure that their execution of this sacrament is exactly how God has called them to exercise this means of God's grace; even if that differs greatly from another church body. At the end of the day, each of us needs to remember that no matter

84

how we interpret our theology it is imperfect at best, as we are imperfect. It is only through God's justification of us through Christ Jesus that we even appear perfect, not by our legalistic interpretations of how we do or do not baptize.

Although I would be presiding at the Eucharist practically every time I lead a worship service, I would only rarely conduct a baptismal service. Baptism would only be offered when it is specifically requested by a patient, staff, or family member. However, even if only done upon request it can still be woven into the liturgy of the pastoral care visit as we gather, share the word, and experience the sacramental blessings that are offered to us.

I have had occasions where parents request baptism for a newborn infant before they ever leave the hospital. I have had occasions where death is imminent for an adult or a newborn, and baptism is requested. I have had occasions where life-changing moments have occurred and baptism is requested. At each of these sacred moments, I remind myself to pause and consider what the person is asking for. Often, baptism is what they are asking for, but on other occasions, it was not, yet it was the only language they knew.

Depending on theology and patient status, baptism can be logistically complicated. But, ignoring the request, no matter the chaplain's theology, is pastorally irresponsible. As a military chaplain, I lean heavily on my colleagues to help me, collectively, to care for individuals under our charge. If someone is requesting baptism or some other sacramental function in a manner or form that is incompatible with the individual chaplain's theology then it is the chaplain's responsibility to help find someone who can accommodate if at all possible.

Logistically for my practices in a hospital setting, I would typically use a kidney basin (small metal or plastic bowl in a kidney shape) filled with warm water (not cold and definitely not hot) and take it to the patient's location. I prepare in advance a brief liturgy and provide copies, if time and logistics allow, for each person present. I encourage the family and friends, staff, and others to attend this celebration of the church as together we worship. We gather, we share the word, and we experience the sacrament.

For infants, I usually encourage one of the parents to hold the child, either standing or sitting. We discuss why we are gathered. We read scripture together and pray. Finally, as the child is baptized small scoops of water are poured over their head from the chaplain's hand.

I had one occasion where an elderly patient was nearing death but had never been baptized. An infection was ravaging her body so all present had to wear protective clothing, gloves, and a mask. The patient herself was barely able to speak and was covered in sores as a result of the infection plaguing her. It was awkward having to take so many precautions for such an intimate act, but her family, some nursing staff, and I gathered at the patient's request for her to be baptized. We gathered in the Triune Name of God, acknowledging our brokenness. We read scripture relating to this sacred moment that brought us together. And, we baptized this child of God shortly before she drew her last breath.

Yet, with the water still glistening on her, and through her pain, she found a moment of peace and solace of her cleanliness. It was a moment of tears and a moment of joy all at one time. Most baptisms are not this dramatic, but I contend that the rejoicing in heaven is equally dramatic each time regardless of the earthly circumstances.

One of the realities of life is that none of us get out of this life alive; we all will die. This may sound quite harsh, but we have the opportunity to normalize and remove the fear from death. We have the opportunity to empower those for whom we care to see it as a natural transition from this life to the next. Especially in a hospital setting, death is a reality we bear witness to frequently. It is often that death or imminent death that draws us to the patient's side bringing words of comfort, hope and peace to the patient, the staff, and the family. We are called on to help them make meaning out of what can seem meaningless and harsh. In these moments we gather, acknowledging and confessing our grief and sorrow. We read and discuss the Word that helps us put in perspective our grief, and reminds us of our hope. But, at this portion of our liturgy where we seek the sacred and tangible things to do I would encourage prayers of commendation, where we commend the dead or dying into the arms of a loving God. At the time of that prayer, we do (if medically allowed) place our hands on the individual, reminiscent of the intimate connection at baptism, and pray prayers of commendation, encouraging family and friends to do the same. It is in this hope that death does lose its sting.

This portion of our liturgy of pastoral care is the portion set aside for something sacred, something where we meet God, something intimate. Although I have been using the term "sacrament" I encourage thinking beyond the legalistic definition or understanding of what a sacrament is or what is sacramental. Here I would encourage the chaplain to consider such things as anointing the sick, foot washing, and laying on of hands or healing touch. In many ways I consider baptism to be a variation of exorcising demons, however, a chaplain may even have exorcism as part of their repertoire as well. As I mentioned previously, this is not an exhaustive representation of what could be offered, but no matter what is offered it should be consistent with the chaplain and the patient's theology, it should be sacred and intimate, and it should be healing and restorative.

Whatever is offered in this "meal" portion of our liturgy needs to be carefully considered. Don't offer things inconsistent with anyone's theology. Don't offer things in an unsafe manner (i.e. candles in a room using oxygen). Don't strong-arm someone into accepting what you are offering, but offer with grace, fully accepting their right to refuse. Be considerate of others in the room, like another patient in the next bed.

No matter how much you desire to fulfill every request personally, you cannot. Yet, this does not let you off the hook from a pastoral care perspective. For instance, I had a Jewish family request to have a Mohel[2] conduct the circumcision of their son in the hospital. As the chaplain I was eager to help facilitate this request, however, my hospital administration and legal department were not as eager. In the Jewish world circumcision is an integral part of faith. In the medical world it is a medical procedure, and having someone who was not a licensed medical provider conduct a medical procedure was simply not going to be allowed in a medical facility. Yet, as their chaplain, I was still eager to walk this journey with them as part of their faith. As the brit milah ("covenant of circumcision") was celebrated in their home I was there with them.

As we transition from this sacred moment we are encouraged, uplifted, and inspired. We feel healing, joy, and hope. It is a moment where God's presence has become tangible to us, and in many ways we feel as Moses did as he visited with the Lord, glowing with God's glory.[3] Not only have we facilitated and led this portion of our liturgy of pastoral care, but we have also participated. Whether it was Holy Communion, Baptism, anointing, or any number of other possibilities our hands were in the midst of what was occurring. The worship was for us too. We too should be singing along with those to whom we minister, "Surely the presence of the Lord is in this place..."[4] as we prepare to depart that time and place of worship.

Other meal practices to consider:

1. Keep available various supplies that may be needed for the more sacramental functions that could arise, even if they are not necessarily part of your tradition. This would be like wine, grape juice, and communion wafers for the Eucharist, or oil for anointing. Appropriate

vessels for this would also be important to have available to you.

2. Have liturgies or orders of service prepared in advance that others can follow along for some of the more common liturgies you may use: baptism, communion, anointing the sick, washing feet, etc.

3. Have a list of other chaplains or clergy readily available who can fill the theological gaps you cannot. As a professional courtesy, ensure that you are also on their list to fill the gaps that may arise for them that you can fill.

The Sending

Most, if not all of us, have had conversations on the phone with a toddler, who seemingly has no concept of phone etiquette. It is not uncommon at all when the toddler is done talking they are truly done, and will happily hang up or just drop the phone in the middle of a sentence. On the other end of that spectrum is the individual who continues a call long after anything meaningful has been said, only repeating what had previously been said out of a refusal to end the call; very much like a filibuster in Congress.

Neither of these is an appropriate way to end a worship service, and neither should they be an appropriate way to end a pastoral care encounter. Yet, many chaplains tend to end pastoral care encounters in this type of destructive manner, derailing the entire pastoral care encounter. They will simply end the visit abruptly as if the time ran out on their clock, or drag it on endlessly from some misguided sense of obligation to stay way beyond their welcome. I propose, however, that if we view our pastoral care encounter in a liturgical framework, in such a way that the sending portion is as integral of a component of our worship as any other part then we will take it more seriously and reverently.

In our liturgical framework what Lutherans typically include in the sending portion of a worship service is very intentional. Included here will be the sending of communion, announcements, a blessing or benediction, a sending song, and a dismissal. Each of these elements has a component of hope, future, and mission woven into their fabric and culminating in a worship experience that honors God and God's people in a blessed communion. They acknowledge the time spent together, but capture the fact that our mission is beyond the church walls.

No matter how ornately or how ordinary a worship space may be in a typical Lutheran church it would be rare to not find the altar and the font prominently placed in the center of what is going on. Also, the pulpit is normally prominently placed and situated, but it is to the side, deferring by its placement to the altar and the font. This is intentional and highlights the importance that is placed on the sacramental portion of our life and worship as a means of God's grace extended to God's people.

Knowing the importance that is placed on Holy Communion, by both the congregation as a whole and its individual members, it is no great surprise that most members greatly desire to receive the sacrament even when they are not able to make it to a worship service. When they receive the bread and wine of the Eucharistic meal, in fact, the same bread and wine their brothers and sisters where they typically worship received, it provides an even greater connectedness to their faith, their faith community, and their God. This extension of the one table, shared even with members unable to participate in person, provides a sense of hope that most would struggle to fully verbalize.

In one of my assignments as a chaplain, I was able to coordinate a lay Eucharistic ministry to help extend our worship to those who were sick and homebound. The congregation, as a whole, became very excited about this ministry opportunity and eagerly sought ways to participate. Even more gratifying was the volunteers' responses to having delivered communion to the sick and shut-in members of the congregation. Many reported back the way that they were even more engaged in the worship experience that occurred as they were visiting in a hospital or nursing home with one who could not attend that week. They shared the scriptures that were read, perhaps songs that were sung, and things they captured from the sermon. They shared the Eucharistic meal and they offered prayers. These volunteers had developed a liturgy of their own centered around a pastoral care experience, and they experienced the worship themselves. They truly understood then that these visits were not putting a check in the box, but also experiencing a moment of worship with one whose body would not allow them to attend.

I have to admit I struggle with announcements in the sending portion of a congregational worship service; they have often felt like a commercial break to me as opposed to a part of the worship. However, as I consider them in the context of this framework of pastoral care I can begin to appreciate them and their placement more. Announcements in a congregation are not for trivial purposes, but missional purposes. The announcements highlight the ministry that the congregation is supporting, praying for, and participating in. They also provide opportunities for the members of the congregation to extend the reach of that congregation to the world around them. As you have been fed and nourished in worship it is good to know what the needs and opportunities in the world are that this worship service has prepared you for.

The benediction is a time of praying on behalf of the congregation and bestowing on them God's blessings. It is a sacred and holy time, reminding the congregation that they are part of one body and blessed in the Triune name of God. The benediction reminds the members of the congregation of their relationship with God, one another, and the world. It is an intentional time of asking God to bless them and their ministry beyond that congregation, both corporately and individually; a lot is happening in what is often one of the shortest prayers of any worship service.

As we part ways at the end of a visit I encourage the chaplain to take this time seriously so that it is the capstone to an already meaningful pastoral care visit. That means considering how we bid farewell to one another with some intentionality that honors the time together, honors our shared faith, and prepares for what comes next.

In a typical church service, the sending liturgy is missional since the congregation is being sent back out into the world on behalf of God and that congregation. They are blessed as they carry communion to the sick and shut-in. They are blessed as they transition to serving in the world beyond the church doors. Even the music is often missional as the members of the congregation lift their voices to God and the world.

Pastoral care visits have a very different tone. Some patients in medical treatment facilities will soon be leaving, and some will not. Inmates in prisons and jails will most likely not be leaving any time soon. However, much of what is embodied in the sending liturgy is an element of hope, promise, and future.

As the sending portion of the pastoral care visit is considered in its whole, the chaplain should seriously contemplate what does hope look like for the individual they are visiting. Hope does not always have a very conventional shape to it, but as Christians, we are truly never without hope, even in circumstances that may seem hopeless.

As previously mentioned, I have personally struggled with the announcements being included in sending part of the liturgy, and I believe an element of that could easily be included with the pastoral care visit. The announcements have the purpose of letting the gathered congregation know what is going on in the life of the congregation: ministries, worship opportunities, transitions, etc. In short, even if individual members would not be participating directly they are encouraged to lift up in prayer the activities going on throughout the congregation.

For a patient or their family spending a few minutes discussing what is coming next could be very helpful. It may be tests or test results, surgery, discharge, therapy, or any of many other possibilities. Each of these can be moments where additional pastoral care would be very appropriate and appreciated. Each of these can be moments where prayer would be sought out. Each of these can be moments of deep and profound emotion that allows the chaplain to help them connect with their faith to find that sense of hope that may not come readily through what the medical provider brings. The peace that a patient or family member can experience when they know that their chaplain will be back at a critical moment or waiting for them on the other end of a procedure may be just the hope that empowers the patient to continue when previously they had lost hope.

Therefore, the announcements that are shared are not just one way, but both ways. The patient and their family share with the chaplain, but also the chaplain should share with the patient and family. When they can expect to see the chaplain again. What other opportunities are available for the patient and family to be spiritually nurtured. In many ways, the exchange of these "announcements" between the chaplain, the patient, and the family serve to further the development of the community. Therefore, as easy as it may be to gloss over this portion of a pastoral care visit, I would advise against it. Doing so can lessen the sense of community, and reduce the hope that can be so vital in many cases; that hope is often the primary element that can further someone's survival.

A sending song may seem a bit unusual for a pastoral care visit. However, its place in the sending liturgy is of profound importance. It is through this song that the community proclaims, in a common voice, their praise of God and their shared mission in the world. Raising the roof with a 100 voice choir and a 268 rank pipe organ may be a bit over the top in a hospital room, but a simple exchange and acknowledgment of God's greatness and the mission we share is not. It is easy for the chaplain to incorporate this into their sending liturgy with a statement of praise of God and the chaplain's ongoing ministry to others that this person who is being visited is an inspiring element of. As the person visited responds, this then becomes their hymn of sending and praise.

One of the final elements in the sending liturgy is the benediction. In a pastoral care visit, this can often feel like the most organic portions of the encounter. The benediction is a blessing, by definition. It is normal for pastoral care visits in hospitals and other institutional settings to conclude with a prayer, but as prayer was discussed earlier, this should not be the only occasion for prayer. Previously we discussed prayers of healing, prayers of invoking God's presence, prayers of the community, etc. I would encourage the chaplain to allow this prayer to intentionally become a prayer of blessing and sending.

For form, there is no specific form. Allow your call and your sense of vocation guide this portion. For many, as in many worship services, the same benediction is used week after week; for others, it varies from week to week. It can be as simple as a genuine and heartfelt, "God bless you," as you shake hands and depart, or as complex and a 4-part, call and response blessing. The beautiful thing is by this point in the pastoral care encounter you have established a rapport and a sense of community, and, as the chaplain, you have a better idea of what the person you are visiting needs. However, it is still very appropriate to ask them directly how you can bless them today. You are not abandoning your pastoral responsibilities to them by pausing and asking how best to serve them and being sensitive to their needs and their boundaries. I would counter, you are being more pastorally caring by ensuring you are meeting their expectations and needs intentionally.

One particular encounter I witnessed that I would not encourage involved a student pastor making visits on behalf of his assigned congregation. He had been instructed to visit all the patients of the local hospital of his faith group, which he was faithfully and somewhat blindly doing. As one of the hospital chaplains, I was visiting the family of one of "his" patients who had died. The patient was still in the hospital bed while the family gathered around his body to say their respective goodbyes. The student pastor came into the room without checking with any hospital staff or even acknowledging my presence as a hospital chaplain making a visit. He brusquely entered the room announcing which church he was representing then went on with, "Oh, I can see Mr. Smith is sleeping." I interrupted him and gently informed him that I was one of the hospital chaplains and that Mr. Smith was, in fact, dead, and I was visiting at the family's request. The student pastor then went into somewhat of a frenzy of apology, mentioned not having his occasional rites materials with him, and flailing around launched into prayer. Following his prayer, he could not leave the room fast enough. If it were not so embarrassing it would have been comical. This also points to the importance of situational awareness before entering any room; it can make the difference between an incredible visit or an incredibly hurtful one.

Now, the chaplain and the patient both, having worshipped together can "Go in peace and serve the Lord." It is a very "churchy" way to say goodbye, but it is a missional way to say goodbye. You are parting not to just go on with your next appointment, but with God's mission to God's people in mind. As you dismiss from one another / say goodbye, keep this in mind. You have been together in worship throughout your visit; therefore even your goodbye should reflect that part of the liturgy. Now you, and those you have visited move on to serve and live out your calling in Christ.

Other Sending practices to consider:

1. Many oncology departments that I have visited, or similar treatment facilities, will often have a symbolic bell that can be rung as a patient completes their chemo or is declared in remission, or even as a patient dies. There is no reason to not include this as part of a pastoral care liturgy, to solemnize the occasion and recognize the presence of the Holy among you. Develop a "bell ringing" liturgy of your own.

2. Nurses, doctors, and other medical professionals tend to come and go frequently with little or no notice. Pausing

for a moment to incorporate a sending and God speed to the individual in recognition for the ministry they offered can prove sacred and meaningful to patients, staff, and families.

Serving and Living

Worship is not, nor should it ever be a show. Neither should worship be simply putting a check in a box of some obligation to complete. We began this discussion considering the role that worship plays between God and God's people. It is relational. It is foundational. And, it is missional. Worship feeds us that we may feed others.

We gather in community for worship, and it is the clergy's responsibility to facilitate that worship; it is our call. This liturgy we have been exploring is but a structure, and a suggested one at that, to reframe the way that we look at our pastoral care encounters. I am not proposing that we all become Lutheran like myself. What I am proposing is that we do not look at our pastoral care encounters as just one of those things we are required to do. Instead, allow it to be one of those things we are allowed, encouraged, and even called to do, leading our community of faith in worship.

101

For me, thinking of my pastoral care visits in a liturgical framework is helpful. It helps me to be mindful that each moment and each element of each visit can be and should be meaningful in our relationship with each other and our relationship with God. I, as a chaplain, have the chance to bring hope to the hopeless, and healing to the wounded; and, I get to do so in God's name.

I mentioned Will Willimon's book earlier, <u>Worship As Pastoral Care</u>[1], and I want to highlight that again. Throughout his book, he highlighted the way that the pastor is caring for his or her congregation through worship, effectively through the teaching and preaching that the pastor is caring for their congregation's pastoral care needs. I would counter that the opposite is also true in that through the pastoral care encounter the chaplain is providing the worship experience to their people. This is an occasion of not "either/or", but "both/and"; worship leads to pastoral care, and pastoral care leads to worship.

In the same vein, as the pastor/chaplain is reframing the pastoral care visit as an act of worship they have the opportunity to address their worshipping community helping them to see and appreciate pastoral care visits they may receive, request, or even participate in as acts of worship. The richness and fullness that can develop in a worshipping community and its individuals by reframing how we envision what a pastoral care visit is can certainly take a community's faith to a new level.

One of my most beloved seminary professors was Dr. Daryl "Tony" Everett[2], an astute and gifted pastoral care professor. One of his coined phrases that permeated our seminary campus was,

"Where is God in all this," (WIGIAT). Not a day goes by that I do not ponder that question, and I continue to ponder it in my pastoral care encounters. I ponder it now as I put an additional framework around my pastoral care encounters and seem them in the context of worship, with an associated liturgy. For me, I can state with certainty that God is right here with us, in the midst of all this, as chaplain and patient gather amongst IV drips, and noisy hospital equipment, with life hanging in the balance for worship.

God welcomes our worship and joins us in it. This is WIGIAT whether life is beginning, life is ending, or somewhere in between. This gives us hope, no matter what. Our God is with us. Amen.

———————————

A timely afterthought and reflection:

Today, April 1, 2020, as I was preparing to make the final touches on this book and submit it for publication, current events gave me pause. Across our nation and our world COVID-19 or The Corona Virus is ravaging our land. People are succumbing to its terrible effects in droves and each day greater restrictions on our liberties are being imposed to help stem the tide of this terrible disease. We are overwhelmed with unsettling news and the fear that it is generating.

From a pastoral care perspective, this disease and world-wide health crisis have had tremendous impact. I can no longer visit my people who are incarcerated or in the hospital with the same freedom I previously took for granted. I cannot hold my people's hands as they cry or to pray with them. I cannot offer a hug to someone in grief. Even our worship has taken a hit; at this point corporate worship has not occurred, by and large, across our country for the last 3 weeks with no projected end in sight when we will be able to gather as God's people again. We are anticipating celebrating Easter, The Resurrection of Our Lord, in isolation from one another as if we were still in the tomb. Yet, I can still interact with and provide pastoral care to my people, and there may even be a liturgy or pattern to this care. But, what would a liturgy of pastoral care look like in a time of national or international crisis?

I met with a young Sailor today experiencing genuine fear and anxiety over this situation we are facing. He was concerned about being separated from his family due to his military obligations. He was concerned about either his family contracting this disease or doing so himself. Most startling to me, however, he was also concerned about the perceptions of other based on his ethnicity; my young Sailor is of Asian heritage.

Real or perceived, he was concerned about racist individuals or groups singling him or his family out, accusing them of having brought this disease to our country. He was genuinely afraid that he would be targeted for acts of hatred due to his ethnicity. As sad as it is, I have to acknowledge that his fear could be well-founded, and there are certainly some who would blame him strictly based on his ethnicity without knowing anything about him as a person.

In the word portion of the liturgy he and I shared today, we discussed his faith, and God's presence with him throughout this challenge and his fears. I did not dismiss his fear, but instead helped him to put his fear in the hands of a loving God by giving him the opportunity to say outloud what was weighing heavily on him. We discussed, very frankly, how God has given us the freedom to choose to do good or the freedom to do evil, and we have no control over those who choose to do evil. Yet, the love that he is able to exhibit by choosing to do good is what he can control, and through his own choices of good experience greater peace because he will not be trying to control others and their choices.

I have reflected on my conversation with him all day since he and I met, and have come to the conclusion that he and I did experience a moment of worship together. He was given the opportunity to confess his fears, and for him this was a shortcoming, and hear in return that God accepts and acknowledges his fear. Together, we spoke of our faith, his and mine, our life, our fears, and our resources for such a time as this.

His circumstances have continued to resonate with me, and from the time of our encounter earlier today I have reflected on his story, his fears, and his faith. His story, and his faithfulness, remind me of one of Jesus' Beatitudes from the Sermon on the Mount as Jesus was speaking to a community who also experienced fear of persecution. Jesus proclaimed, "Blessed are you when people revile you and persecute you and utter all kinds of evil against you falsely on my account. Rejoice and be glad, for your reward is great in heaven, for in the same way they persecuted the prophets who were before you."[3] We cannot control the hatred that people will have for us, even in the midst of a crisis. People may hate simply because of who we are or who we are not, but we are still blessed. People will target us because of our race, our gender, our age, or whatever, but we are still blessed. I trust that God's people are a faithful and resilient people, and despite our current circumstances that most will choose to do good and not evil; most will choose to love.

Although not said in so many words, I effectively sent him forth with that same admonition, "Blessed are you...". And, I did witness peace in his countenance as he went on his way. Helping him to see the way that God is blessing him and others in the midst of this chaos settled many of his fears and gave him the peace he needed to go forth.

There was no formal liturgy between us, but a liturgy was still present as we worshiped and shared together. We gathered and greeted one another, and confessed what weighs us down. We shared the word, the story of our lives, and the word, God's story in our midst. Because of what we are calling "social distancing" we were not able to share a sacramental element, or meal, of our time together, but we did intentionally part with a blessing of sending. This was our liturgy for a time of crisis.

In moments of crisis, like COVID-19, like 9/11, like December 7th 1941, or like so many more occasions, the most healing thing we have to offer through our liturgy is peace. We cannot control the chaos, but we can offer genuine love and peace for those who need it most; including ourselves.

So, Chaplain, Blessed are you too!

Boundaries

As a final word, I do need to discuss boundaries. One of the greatest tools of love, respect, and safety are our boundaries. Even if we do not acknowledge them and claim to be an "open book," we have boundaries. The same is true for those we are called upon to care for. As a pastoral care provider, it should be central to our care that we are attentive to those boundaries and do all we can to protect them; including our own.

Think of boundaries pastorally in the same way that we think of physical boundaries. We have boundaries around our homes and property that we expect others to gain permission before crossing. We have boundaries in our finances where we expect others to pay us what they owe us. We have boundaries around our hearts as well, and we expect those to be respected too. The challenge is the fact that these boundaries are less tangible and not universally considered; so we must become aware. Yet, the saying that, "fences make good neighbors," is equally apt in pastoral care.

One boundary in worship and congregations that is broken most frequently is personal space. The sharing of the peace is such an integral part of worship that many cannot conceive of doing without it. Symbolically and literally, it is the reconciliation of the people, forgiving one another any real or perceived sins, before dining together at our Lord's table. However, in practice, it varies wildly from one congregation to the next as to how "enthusiastic" that sharing of peace may become.

In some congregations the sharing may be little more than the presiding minister announcing, "May the peace of Christ be with you all," with the congregation responding, "And, also with you;" yet no physical contact ever takes place. The other end of the extreme is a full-body embrace by every member of the congregation with every other member of the congregation; often lasting quite some time. Along that continuum exists the reality of every congregation with which I have ever worshiped.

The challenge with this practice is not with the normal worshipers that are part of that family every time they gather, but with the visitor who does not know the ways of that congregation. I have seen the anxiety so high in some visitors approaching the time of the sharing of the peace that they will either leave the worship before it begins or conveniently need to visit the restroom then. When this occurs, we are not considering boundaries and are hurting people. The same can occur in pastoral care settings.

When we enter someone's "space," be that their home or hospital room, we should recognize the fact that we have been invited to cross a boundary already, and begin to look for other boundaries that we may soon cross; we are the visitor into their world. Some I have visited have resisted vehemently being touched in any way, while others practically insist on a hug and holding my hand throughout the visit. An attentive pastoral care provider should notice readily the inclinations of the person being visited, but if you are still not certain then become comfortable with asking.

Some visits, however, it is neither the patient nor the chaplain's preference for the boundaries, but medical orders and necessity. Someone who is on contact precautions cannot be touched casually. It does not matter if the invader to their space is their doctor, their nurse, the spouse, or their chaplain; all must wear appropriate protective clothing and refrain from unnecessary touching. This is as much to protect the patient as it is the visitor and others they may come in contact with.

I've experienced similarly imposed separation in visiting people who have been incarcerated. Although as a chaplain I do tend to get a freer opportunity to visit people than most, I still am often relegated to visiting through 2 inch thick glass and speaking on a phone. It is horribly impersonal, but we can still make the content of our encounter meaningful.

Boundaries from one patient to the next can easily make a pastoral care provider's head spin. I have personally experienced this the most in labor and delivery wards, and post partum wards.

New mothers are all over the charts as to how welcoming of a pastoral care visit they may be or how resistant. I have been visiting with a new mother and she ask me to leave in order to breast feed, and then with others who say nothing to me at all before bearing their breast and beginning to nurse their baby. Oddly, I did not find this uncomfortable and was able to easily continue my visit. However, a chaplain colleague of mine became very anxious over the same situation. This is where our own boundaries begin to come into play.

Pastoral care providers need to become comfortable with being assertive in their own level of comfort and vulnerability that they can endure. If they do not, then the poison of the anxiety that they experience will end up compromising the pastoral care visit.

For me personally, the most unusual and uncomfortable visit was to a patient hospitalized for gastro-intestinal concerns. As I knocked and entered her room I was invited in by a room full of people, with the exception of the patient herself. I assumed that she had been taken for some procedure or testing but her family assured me she was present as they pointed to the open restroom door. And, there she was, sitting on the toilet. She then engaged me in a truly unusual dialogue and eventually asked me to pray for her as she continued her "business" on the toilet. I drew the line at walking into the restroom with her, but I did raise my voice to be heard, by her and God, and offered a prayer for her. I then quickly exited her room; I had found my boundary. I believe my visit was effective for her, to some degree, however, because I was not assertive about my own boundaries the pastoral care visit was not as effective as it could have been. This, was a lesson learned for me.

As you make pastoral care visits, please be attentive to boundaries. Notice the boundaries of your patients. Notice the boundaries of the medical, assisted care, jail/prison, or other staff. Notice the boundaries of your church body. But also, notice your own boundaries. If you do not pay attention to these then you are not extending the fullest care possible, and you are not including yourself in the encounter.

On the other hand, it is also very appropriate to push, certain, boundaries; especially our own. This is at the heart of the CPE experience, as previously mentioned. We are people too, and we experience fear and apprehensions. We also have our own baggage from our personal history. Not pushing our boundaries to enlarge our comfort zone to more fully embrace the people for whom we care will severely limit their care. However, being too open with our boundaries is just as irresponsible, to ourselves. With counsel, mentorship, prayer, and reflection constantly discern those boundaries that help you to be the best pastoral care provider you can be. These are the fences in our ministry that creates the best neighbors.

Acknowledgments

The seeds of this book began during the year I was fortunate enough to participate in a pastoral care residency program. It was a full-time, intensive year of study, reflection, and practice, completing four units of Clinical Pastoral Education (CPE). The program I participated in was part of my career as a Navy chaplain and conducted jointly through the Naval Medical Center Portsmouth in Portsmouth, VA, and the Veterans' Affairs Hospital in Hampton, VA. To say the program left a lasting impact on me and my ministry is an extreme understatement.

The success of the program was primarily due to the efforts of Dr. Kim Nielsen with VA Hospital in Hampton, VA who was our CPE supervisor. He guided our development and helped us to unfold truths about ourselves and our ministry that were often hard for us to grasp. We affectionately referred to him as Gandalf, the bearded, and the wizened wizard in J. R. R. Tolkien's novels The Hobbit and The Lord of the Rings, who served as a guide for those finding, seeking, and protecting the ring. To my cohort in my pastoral care residency program, we felt as though Dr. Nielsen was our Gandalf for his wisdom, his "wizardliness", and especially his dashing beard. I could never possibly thank him enough for his patience and his wisdom during that very formative year for me. He not only allowed me but encouraged me continuously to "use your dumber side."

Included in my Pastoral Care Residency cohort were three other Navy chaplains and a Canadian Army chaplain: Michael

113

Chaney, Jeffrey Bornemann, Jon Rozema, and David Stewart. At every turn, these four gentlemen pushed me, challenged me, and stretched me in ways I was not expecting. Never were they unkind, but they never accepted "bare minimum" or "just getting by" level of work. Together we struggled through many things that hampered our ministry, and through that struggle opened new ways of caring for people we had never thought of before.

The Pastoral Care Residency was the catalyst that launched me to consider my provision of pastoral care in new and novel ways, going beyond where I had always gone. In this time the seed was planted to begin to see our provision of pastoral care as worship. As depicted in the encounter between Jesus and a Samaritan woman getting water in the Gospel of John, there has been and continues to be a proclivity to thinking in narrow terms about where we can and should worship: "The woman said to [Jesus], 'Sir, I see that you are a prophet. Our ancestors worshiped on this mountain, but you say that the place where people must worship is in Jerusalem.'"[1] Jesus' astonishing response removed that restraint and understanding with, "Woman, believe me, the hour is coming when you will worship the Father neither on this mountain nor in Jerusalem."[2] Our worship should not be constricted to one set location or venue, but to inhabit the entirety of our lives; including our homes, our hospital rooms, our prison cells, or wherever we may be. Now, I feel more connected with the whole of my life as a continuous act of worship with an incredible cloud of witnesses gathered around me.

During my residency, I read from three authors whose work stood out helping me to see the appropriateness of our pastoral care encounters as worship events: Elaine Ramshaw[3], Gordon W. Lathrop[4], and William H. Willimon[5]. Each inspired me to begin to see our pastoral care encounters differently and more intentionally. I trust their body of work will continue to inspire others long after me in how we see our worship and our pastoral care intertwining.

The beginning of my vocabulary for all that pastoral care encompasses is squarely in the teaching and mentoring of Dr. Daryl "Tony" Everett. He is beyond compare in his shaping of generations of pastors and unleashing them in the world, prepared to serve their congregations and communities of faith with a well-formed sense of what pastoral care is. He gave me the language to begin to even ask the right questions.

Finally, without the influence and strong determination of the Reverend Dr. C. Peter Setzer, I am confident that I would not have taken God's call to me to consider ordained ministry seriously. He baptized my wife, he presided at our wedding, he celebrated with us at moments of celebration and wept with us at moments of grief. In short, he was my first real model of what pastoral care looks like. He had seen in me something that I could not see myself and refused to take "No" for an answer. Yet he patiently stood by me and helped me to discern this wonderful calling that has allowed me to enter into the incredible inner sanctum of so many people's lives. I can never thank him enough for loving God, God's people, and me enough to believe that I

115

could do this. I never dreamed that I could love doing something as much as I loved being an engineer, but I love this even more.

About the Author

John Connolly is an ordained Lutheran pastor (minister of word and sacrament) in the Evangelical Lutheran Church in America (ELCA) and currently serves as a chaplain in the US Navy. As part of his seminary education and church requirements, he completed a unit of Clinical Pastoral Education (CPE) at Moses Cone Hospital in Greensboro, NC. Also, together with other chaplains while stationed at the US Naval Academy, he completed another unit of CPE. However, the Navy offered him as one of his assignments the opportunity to participate in a joint program between the US Navy Chaplain Corps and the Department of Veterans Affairs Chaplaincy program that is a year-long Pastoral Care Residency, completing four additional units of CPE, which is part of the Navy Chaplain Corps' Advanced Education Program. After completing this program in Portsmouth, VA he subsequently completed a hospital assignment at Naval Hospital Jacksonville in Jacksonville, FL. Although these two Naval Hospital assignments along with his previous CPE experience certainly provided the catalyst inspiring and completing this project, it was the combination of all of his assignments and training, Navy and civilian, which helped bring this book to fruition. He also published, "The Just War Tradition: A Model For Healthcare Ethics" in the HEC Forum (Healthcare Ethics Committee Forum) in 2018, inspired by his work in Navy Medicine.

In addition to his hospital assignments, he has served in other Navy and Marine Corps assignments, including Marine Corps Recruit Depot Parris Island, the USS Harpers Ferry, the USS Germantown, the USS George H W Bush, and the US Naval Academy in Annapolis, MD where he learned the Navy's fabled and often repeated liturgy, "Go Navy! Beat Army!"

John grew up in Gastonia, NC and enlisted in the Navy's Delayed Entry Program during his senior year of high school and shortly after graduation reported for duty. He earned a degree in electrical engineering following his six-year enlistment in the Navy, and worked as an electrical engineer specializing in industrial automation in the Charlotte, NC area for the next 15 years before wrestling with God's call in his life to consider ordained ministry and subsequently going to seminary. Following seminary and ordination, he was offered the opportunity to return to the Navy as a chaplain, which he eagerly accepted.

He credits his wife, Emma, and her adventurous spirit that not only allowed him to leave a steady and prosperous job as an engineer to go to seminary and return to the Navy as a chaplain but eagerly encouraged it. However, their greatest joy together now is enjoying seeing the beautiful young woman their daughter,

Maggie, is becoming, and both believe that being her parents is the adventure and call of a lifetime.

Bibliography

Barbieri, C. (2018). Praying the Scriptures: An Introduction to the History and Practice of Lectio Divinia. Digital Deacon Ministries.

Bennett, G. (1978). When They Ask for Bread: Or, Pastoral Care and Counseling in Everyday Places. Louisville, KY: Westminster John Knox Press.

Colbert, D. (2003). Deadly Emotions: Understand The Mind-Body-Spirit Connection That Can Heal Or Destroy You. Nashville: Thomas Nelson Publishers.

Division of Christian Education of the National Council of the Churches of Christ in the United States of America. (1989). *The Bible* (New Revised Standard Version ed.). Nashville, TN: Thomas Nelson Publishers.

Kolb, R., & Wengert, T. J. (Eds.). (2000). *The Book of Concord: The Confessions of the Evangelical Lutheran Church.* (C. Arand, E. Gritsch, R. Kolb, W. Russell, J. Schaaf, J. Strohl, & T. J. Wengert, Trans.) Minneapolis: Fortress Press.

Lathrop, G. W. (2011). *The Pastor: A Spirituality.* Minneapolis: Fortress Press.

Morehead, P. D., & Morehead, A. T. (Eds.). (2006). *The New American Webster Handy College Dictionary* (4th ed.). New York: New American Library, a division of Penguin Group (USA).

Morehead, P. D., & Morehead, A. T. (Eds.). (2006). *The New American Webster Handy College Dictionary* (4th ed.). New York: New American Library, a division of Penguing Group (USA).

Nouwen, H. J. (1975). Reaching Out: The Three Movements Of The Spiritual Life. New York: Doubleday.

Nouwen, H. J. (1979). *The Wounded Healer.* New York: Doubleday.

Ramshaw, E. (1987). *Ritual and Pastoral Care.* (D. S. Browning, Ed.) Philadelphia: Fortress Press.

The Use of the Means of Grace: A Statement on the Practice of Word and Sacrament. (1997). Minneapolis: Augsburg Fortress.

Warren, T. H. (2016). Liturgy of the Ordinary: Sacred Practices in Everyday Life. Westmont, Illinois: IVP Books.

Willimon, W. H. (1979). *Worship As Pastoral Care.* Nashville: Abingdon Press.

Wolf, L. (Composer). (1977). Surely the Presence of the Lord Is in This Place. Cleveland, TN: Pathway Music.

Notes

What is Pastoral Care?

---

[1] Typical saying of Dr. Kim Nielsen, Hampton VA Medical Center, Hampton, VA, CPE Supervisor
[2] (Nouwen H. J., 1979, p. 92)
[3] 1 Corinthians 13:4-7
[4] Exodus 3:1-7

Why We Have Pastoral Care?

[1] (Colbert, 2003, p. 64)
[2] (Nouwen H. J., 1975, pp. 71-72)

What is Worship?

[1] (Morehead & Morehead, The New American Webster Handy College Dictionary, 2006)
[2] Matthew 16:13b-14
[3] Matthew 16:15b-16
[4] Genesis 1:26
[5] Genesis 17:7
[6] Genesis 9:13
[7] 1 Corinthians 11:25
[8] John 3:35
[9] John 14:30a
[10] John 15:13
[11] (Kolb & Wengert, 2000, p. 23)
[12] The "filioque" controversy developed over the addition of the phrase "and the Son" to the 3rd article by the Western Church / Roman Catholic Church without consulting the Eastern Church near the end of the 1st millennium. The Western Church and subsequent Protestant Churches that have come from the Western Church still use the Nicene Creed including the controversial phrase, and the Eastern Church still does not include it.
[13] Mark 10:45
[14] Matthew 18:20
[15] (Morehead & Morehead, The New American Webster Handy College Dictionary, 2006)

What is Liturgy?

[1] (Warren, 2016)
[1] Exodus 3:11b
[2] Exodus 3:13b
[3] Exodus 3:14
[4] Isaiah 6:5-7
[5] Exodus 20:7
[6] Genesis 18:1-15
[7] Matthew 11:28-30
[8] Association of Evangelical Lutheran Churches, Lutheran Church in America, The American Lutheran Church, The Evangelical Lutheran Church of Canada, 1982
[9] Matthew 16:18-19
[10] Leviticus 20:10
[11] John 8:1-11
[12] (Bennett, 1978)

The Word

[1] *Ko amar Adonai*, a typical saying prefacing many prophecies in the Old Testament means, "Thus says the Lord."
[2] (Ramshaw, 1987, p. 55)
[3] (Barbieri, 2018)
[4] Exodus 15:1-18
[5] 1 Samuel 16:23

The Meal

[1] (The Use of the Means of Grace: A Statement on the Practice of Word and Sacrament, 1997)
[2] A Mohel is an individual trained and authorized within the Jewish community to provide the rite of circumcision, consistent with the Jewish faith.
[3] See Exodus 34:29-35
[4] (Wolf, 1977)

Serving and Living

[1] (Willimon, 1979)

[2] Rev. Daryl "Tony" Everett, Th.D, retired Professor of Pastoral Care, Lutheran Theological Southern Seminary, Columbia, SC

[3] Matthew 5:11-12

Acknowledgments

[1] John 4:19-20
[2] John 4:21
[3] (Ramshaw, 1987)
[4] (Lathrop, 2011)
[5] (Willimon, 1979)

www.ingramcontent.com/pod-product-compliance
Lightning Source LLC
Chambersburg PA
CBHW031553040426
42452CB00006B/297